Ball Pythons

Colette Sutherland

Ball Pythons

Project Team
Editor: Thomas Mazorlig
Copy Editor: Joann Woy
Indexer: Ann W. Truesdale
Series Design: Mary Ann Kahn
Design: Patti Escabi

TFH Publications®
President/CEO: Glen S. Axelrod
Executive Vice President: Mark E. Johnson
Editor-in-Chief: Albert Connelly, Jr.
Production Manager: Kathy Bontz

TFH Publications, Inc.®
One TFH Plaza
Third and Union Avenues
Neptune City, NJ 07753

13 14 15   9 10 11 8

ISBN 978-0-7938-2859-3

Library of Congress Cataloging-in-Publication Data
Sutherland, Colette.
  Ball pythons : a complete guide to Python regius / Colette Sutherland.
     p. cm.
  Includes index.
  ISBN 978-0-7938-2859-3 (alk. paper)
  1. Ball pythons as pets. I. Title.
  SF459.S5C655 2009
  639.3'9678—dc22
                                        2008054754

This book has been published with the intent to provide accurate and authoritative information in regard to the subject matter within. While every reasonable precaution has been taken in preparation of this book, the author and publisher expressly disclaim responsibility for any errors, omissions, or adverse effects arising from the use or application of the information contained herein. The techniques and suggestions are used at the reader's discretion and are not to be considered a substitute for veterinary care. If you suspect a medical problem consult your veterinarian.

The Leader In Responsible Animal Care For Over 50 Years!®
www.tfh.com

Table of Contents

Chapter 1

Natural History

Many people purchase a reptile for a pet with little or no understanding of that particular animal's native range, habits, or vital statistics. Understanding a small portion of the reptile's natural history may help to explain some of its habits. Being aware of the reptile's size, maximum length, longevity, and other factors will help you determine if the particular animal you are considering purchasing will be a good choice for your circumstances.

Range and Habitat

Ball pythons are native to West and Central Africa. This large area consists primarily of coastal African countries, with the ball python's range extending into a few interior countries such as Chad, Sudan, Mali, and the Central African Republic. It is interesting to note that the geographic range of the ball python does not extend below the equator into the southern hemisphere.

The preferred habitat of the ball python is grasslands and savannas, although they sometimes are found in forested areas. In grasslands, ball pythons can occasionally be found living in termite mounds, although they are more likely to live in rodent burrows—where it's highly likely that the previous owner of the burrow became a meal for the ball python. It is not uncommon to find more than one python in a burrow; however, once females begin to brood their eggs, males do not stay in the burrow with them. Occasionally, more than one brooding female may inhabit a burrow, possibly because of a lack of good nesting spots in a given area.

Ball pythons do not appear to be disturbed by the activities of man and are common in agricultural areas. There's rarely a shortage of rodents in farm land, so it makes sense that, with this great abun-

Ball pythons are native to the savannas of Africa, being found south of the Sahara and north of the equator.

Ball Python Origins

Map showing approximate natural range of the ball python (black) and the range of the closely related Angolan python (green).

dance of available food, the ball python would be there to exploit it.

Since ball pythons range fairly close to the equator, they experience very little variance in their light cycle on an annual basis; the closer to the equator, the more equal are the lengths of day and night during the entire year. The average temperature in the area that they inhabit is also fairly warm, with some areas having an annual average temperature of as high as 85°F (29.4°C). The grasslands and savannas where ball pythons live also experience two distinct seasons, wet and dry. The dry season generally lasts from November through April. It is important to note that ball python eggs begin to hatch at the beginning of the wet season, when food is more plentiful and humidity

The Father of Taxonomy

Carl Linnaeus developed the modern taxonomic system in 1758, in the tenth edition of his *Systema Naturae*. He standardized the use of binomial nomenclature (assigning two names to each species), and he used a classification system that ranked species by their similarities.

is very high. The dry season sees very little rain, but humidity may still be as high as 80 percent.

Wild Collection

Three of the 12 coastal countries where ball pythons are found—Ghana, Togo, and Benin—are the largest exporters of these pythons into the United States. Each year, trappers who specialize in this activity collect ball python eggs. They bring these eggs into large holding facilities where they are held until they hatch. Once the eggs have hatched, hatchlings by the hundreds are prepared for shipment to various countries. Thousands arrive each year into the United States. Unfortunately, many adults are also shipped into the United States each year, and a percentage of these are gravid females. In the past, these adult snakes have not done very well in captivity. Many of them refuse to eat and eventually perish. The hatchlings, on the other hand, generally do very well and can go on to live in captivity for many years with proper care.

Taxonomy

Taxonomy is the system used by scientists to classify living organisms into similar or related groups. As science and technology progress and information increases, so do the methods used to determine relationships among organisms. DNA analysis, something that was unavailable years ago, is now more commonly used to determine how living organisms are related to one another. Earlier methods for classifying snakes that are still used today include scale counts, bone structure, and other anatomical characteristics. These methods can be confusing, because we don't usually know what characteristics developed first or which ones are truly the most important in determining relationships. The advent of DNA analysis allows

Ball pythons being collected from the wild for the pet trade.

much greater accuracy in classification.

All living organisms have two names: the common name and the scientific name. Common names are the familiar, everyday names of living things, such as dog, leopard gecko, and ball python. Scientific names are written in Latinized form—some of the names are truly Latin while others are Latin versions of words from other languages. Most early scientific texts

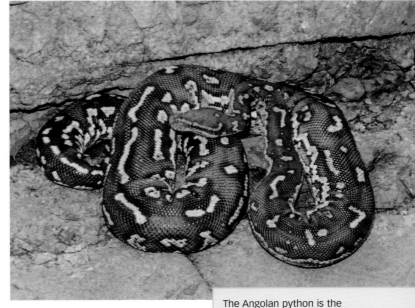

The Angolan python is the closest living relative of the ball python. It inhabits a small range in Namibia and Angola.

were written in Latin, and because of this, when a species was named, the Latin language was used. The continued use of Latin persists, since this provides for continuity among various scientific texts and journals. Regardless of which country you live in or which language you speak, the scientific or Latin name for a specific plant or animal will always be the same.

Ball pythons belong to the family Pythonidae, although some authorities consider this a subfamily of Boidae, the boas. This family is further broken down into eight genera (the plural of genus; genus is the level of classification just above species): *Antaresia* (dwarf Australian pythons), *Aspidites* (black-headed pythons and woma pythons), *Bothrochilus* (Bismarck ringed python), *Leiopython* (white-lipped python), *Liasis* (olive, Macklot's, water pythons, and relatives), *Apodora* (Papuan python), *Morelia* (carpet, diamond, green tree, Boelen's, and amethystine pythons), and *Python* (Burmese, blood, rock, reticulated, and similar species). Ball pythons belong to the genus *Python*, which also contains the largest of the world's python species. The other members of *Python* are the reticulated, African rock, Timor, blood, Indian (including the Burmese subspecies), and Angolan pythons. The Angolan python (*P. anchietae*) is the ball python's closest relative. The ball python is the smallest member of this genus, rarely exceeding 6.5 feet (2 m) in total length.

The ball python's scientific name is *Python regius*. Literally translated, it means "royal python." (In Europe, *P. regius* is known as the royal python, while in America it is called the ball python.) It is possible that this small python received its scientific name in part because of the number of African tribes that worshipped it. In many areas of Africa, the ball python is still considered a sacred animal. In some older literature, *P. regius* is referred to as the regal python.

Description

Ball pythons are fairly short, heavy-bodied snakes. Their average length is between 4 and 5 feet (1.2 and 1.5 m). They are muscular, with a well-defined, slender neck. The head is narrow at the nose and broader at the base of the skull. Five labial heat-sensing pits are located on each side of the upper jaw; these are used to sense infrared radiation (body heat) given off by prey. These labial pits are able to detect small variations in temperature of only a few degrees. Keep this in mind when feeding your snake frozen thawed rodents by hand; if your hand is giving off more heat than the food item, chances are you will be bitten.

The small holes in the lips of ball pythons—seen here on a hypomelanistic one—are actually heat-sensing organs used to detect warm-blooded prey.

The normal appearance of a wild ball pythons is generally a black or dark brown background color with lighter blotches of either gold or light brown. The pattern is highly variable. Individuals can be striped, blotched, banded, or a combination of all three patterns. The ventral surface or belly of the ball python is generally white, with occasional black or yellow flecking. Like fingerprints, no two ball pythons have an identical pattern, even when

Herp-Eat-Herp World

The number of large animals in Africa has declined over the years. Many of them exist primarily in large wildlife parks. The number of small animals has not fared much better, since many of them are used for food for both humans and other animals. This has most likely left the ball python with fewer predators than it had to deal with historically. Today, it is most likely that the ball python's biggest predators are other reptiles. The savanna monitor and three species of cobra share the ball python's habitat. The savanna monitor is an opportunistic feeder, and it is doubtful that it will reject the opportunity to slurp down an unsuspecting ball python. Cobras are known to be snake eaters, and they occupy the same types of burrows as ball pythons, so it is highly likely that the cobra, too, would not turn down the opportunity to eat a ball python.

they hatch from the same egg. Many times, the lighter areas on the ball python will contain dark markings. At times, when these markings or spots are nearer the top of the pattern, it gives the blotch the appearance of being in the form of strange "face," similar to the purported faces of space aliens. Many people refer to this type of pattern as "aliens" markings.

Ball pythons, whether male or female, have cloacal spurs—small stubs on either side of the cloaca. Males use these spurs during courtship. Occasionally, the spurs may wear down and may even break off. You cannot tell the sex of a ball python by the size of the spurs.

Ball pythons are most active at night, when they emerge from their burrows to go foraging for food or looking for a mate. When you keep one, you will notice that as the lights go off, it will not be long before your ball python will come out and crawl around its enclosure.

In the wild, ball pythons eat a variety of animals, from birds to bats to small mammals. One study found that ball pythons less than 30 inches (76.2 cm) long primarily fed on birds, while ball pythons over 39 inches (99.1 cm) in the same area fed primarily on small mammals. This is not an unusual occurrence in nature. Many species of animals will prey on different types of food items depending upon their size or even their sex.

Because the ball python's primary habitat is the savanna, there is little opportunity for this species to climb, given that most savannas have very few trees. It is possible that ball pythons inhabiting areas with more trees have more opportunities to exercise their climbing potential. In general though, with the exception of an occasional climb, ball pythons are not built for life in the trees. All ball pythons are good swimmers.

Chapter 2

Pet Considerations

Out of all the boas and pythons, ball pythons make the best pets for the average keeper. They stay relatively small and are not prone to aggression. Their care is relatively undemanding; most keepers will have little difficulty providing one with a proper captive environment. While wild-caught adults have a reputation for refusing food, captive-bred hatchlings feed reliably and become interesting and docile pets.

Prior to the 1990s, ball pythons were considered problematic and extremely difficult to keep alive. During this time, many ball pythons died as a result of failure to feed. The only snakes available then were imported animals, usually adults. Adults rarely acclimated and many perished.

It was difficult for most of these adults to acclimate due to lack of general knowledge of parasite loads and proper ways to set them up to decrease their stress from being imported. Many wild-caught adults would not eat for up to a year! Only those hobbyists with lots of patience were able to work successfully with these adults. When the techniques used by these few people were shared with others, more and more people began to understand how to properly take care of imported adults. Many adults are still brought into the country today, and these adults can be a problem for those who do not know how to care for them.

As their common name suggests, ball pythons curl up into a ball when they feel threatened.

As hobbyists increased their knowledge about the care requirements of ball pythons, diligent and passionate individuals began to successfully breed them in captivity. The first color mutations (called *morphs*) also encouraged more individuals to devote time to the care and reproduction of the ball python. Today, over 100 different colors and patterns are available to choose from, and ball pythons are one of the five most popular reptiles to keep.

Due to their small size and relatively docile nature, ball pythons are one of the best snakes to keep as a pet. It is important to know that ball pythons have a long potential life span. Forty-seven years is the official record for the oldest ball python in captivity; it lived at the Philadelphia Zoo. Since they do have the potential to live such a long time, you must make sure that (to the best of your knowledge) you will be able to provide for the needs of your ball python throughout its life. If for some reason your circumstances change and you are no longer able to care for your pet and are not able to find a suitable home for it, other resources are available to help you. Many herpetological societies across the United States have adoption programs, and many pet shops may be willing to purchase your snake from you. Your local animal shelter may also be able to take your snake if you are no longer able to provide for it. Reptile-related forums on the Internet can also be helpful in trying to find a home for an unwanted ball python. Under no circumstances should you ever release your pet into the wild. Ball pythons do not belong out in the local environment, and it causes tremendous problems when a released snake shows up in an area where it does not belong.

Acquisition

Before you acquire a ball python, make sure you read this entire book through at least once—both for your benefit and that of your snake. After reading the book, you will be able to make an informed decision about whether you will be able care for a ball python, and if so, what preparations are needed before you bring your snake home.

Ball pythons are readily available from a number of different sources. You can purchase one at your local pet shop, local reptile expo, off the Internet, through your local newspaper, or even perhaps through your local herp club. Each potential source of available ball pythons will have its own unique set of pros and cons. You will need to decide which will work best for you.

Adoption

Herpetological societies are not found in every state. Where they are located, however, they provide a great opportunity for people to gather together and share their common interests in reptiles and amphibians. Many of these societies have adoption programs for re-homing reptiles and amphibians whose owners are no longer able to care for them. They also

For the beginning keeper, it is best to purchase a captive-bred ball python that has eaten at least a few meals.

Long-Lived Snakes

A ball python holds the record for the longest-lived snake in captivity. The Philadelphia Zoo received a half-grown ball python and successfully maintained it in their collection for 47 years! Keep this in mind when considering a ball python as a pet—it can be a long-term commitment.

receive animals from local shelters and from local law enforcement agencies. Most clubs will require you to become a member before they will allow you to adopt an animal. There will also most likely be an adoption contract that you will be required to sign before you will be allowed to take the snake home. Each club has its own adoption requirements.

Private Party

Buying from a private party out of the local paper can be a very interesting experience. Most of these snakes will be adult ball pythons. Some will be in excellent health; others will need lots of tender, loving care. (Be sure that, if the python is not in the best of health, you will be able to provide whatever specialized—and probably expensive—care it needs.) Some of these snakes will have belonged to children who have grown up, left home, gone off to college, or who just plain lost interest in their once-beloved pet. Almost all of our original ball python females came from people selling snakes that they no longer wanted to care for.

If you want a ball python of a specific color morph, such as this piebald, you may need to buy directly from a breeder.

Pet Shops

Local pet shops have long been the first place where many future hobbyists encounter their first reptiles. Some stores are very neat and clean, employing knowledgeable staff and offering healthy animals. Others are not as well kept or staffed. At a pet shop, you will have the opportunity to observe an individual snake for a potentially longer period of time then you would at an expo. When you have decided upon which ball python you would like to purchase, please ask to see its feeding record, if one is available, or watch it eat before you bring it home. This is important, since one of the biggest complaints that consistently occur with ball pythons is their failure to feed. Well-cared-for hatchling ball pythons should eat as long as they are properly set up and cared for.

Herp Expo

Ah, a herp expo! For the reptile and amphibian enthusiast, this is the place to be! An expo (also called a herp show), usually held in a public area such as a convention hall, provides a platform for individuals who deal with reptiles, amphibians, and related products to offer them for sale to the public. Not all expos are the same. Some are fairly small and regional, while others are very large and attract breeders and dealers from around the United States.

Buying at an expo gives you an opportunity to inspect a large number of ball pythons. Not all sellers of ball pythons at the expos are breeders. Many are brokers, and others are importers. It is important to take your time and visit a number of vendor's tables and buy a quality, well-started ball python from a reliable seller. If you ask to handle a ball python on a vendor's table, do not be surprised if she asks you to sanitize your hands before allowing you to handle her snakes. (Most vendors carry their own hand sanitizers with them. This is a common practice among vendors.)

Choose the seller that you are most comfortable with. Most important, make sure you obtain the seller's contact information in case there is a problem with the snake or if you have more questions at a later date about the snake you purchased.

Online Sources

The Internet offers hundreds of places where you can purchase ball pythons from breeders, brokers, and importers. Some only care about how much money they can make from the sale of the snake, while others have a passion for the snakes themselves. Before purchasing online, try to obtain references about the seller. This is very important. Many times, buyers shop for the least expensive ball python they can purchase. While this may save money in the short term, it can be quite costly in the long run, in either veterinary bills or in a setback during a breeding project. (For example, if

Captive Bred Is Best

Spending a few dollars more on a quality, captive-bred ball python will reduce the potential for problems with your new pet. They usually are eating regularly and free of parasites. Always have your research completed before you buy, not after. Buying from a reputable breeder or establishment will save you headaches in the future.

Hold the Sympathy

you bought snakes that were supposed to produce albino morph babies, but they only produced normal babies after numerous breeding trials, this would be a huge setback in time and money.) As with any business, there are unscrupulous individuals in the reptile world, so take care when purchasing your ball python.

Most breeders now offer photos of the individual snakes that they have for sale. Along with photos, most will offer records. Some of the information that breeders can supply may include feeding records, hatch date, weights, shed dates, and parental history. Some breeders may offer more complete records than others. The most important information is the parentage, hatch date, and information that would indicate a consistent weight gain since the date of hatching if the feeding records are not completely current.

Purchasing a Healthy Ball Python

Once you have decided where to purchase your snake, the next step is to choose a healthy ball python. When buying over the Internet, you must rely upon the integrity and reputation of the seller, which is why doing your research is so important before you purchase from an online source. If you choose to buy from an expo, pet shop, or private party, you'll want to carefully examine the snake of your choice. Bring your own hand sanitizer. Being prepared is always a good thing, and after handling some snakes, you may really want to sanitize your hands! Some snakes may have skin problems or mites that you do not want on your hands.

Before you purchase a ball python, inspect it carefully for signs of poor health.

A ball python's nostrils should be free of any liquid, discharge, or bubbling noises, all signs of a respiratory infection.

Overall Condition

Regardless of the condition of the snake you are considering, you must handle it. The snake should look alert and flick its tongue while being handled. Handling the snake will allow you to determine its muscle tone and body condition. It should feel firm and muscular. The snake should not feel boney, nor should it feel soft and mushy. Pass on snakes that have poor body condition. Snakes, especially babies, that are not feeding well or that have never fed will feel soft and have poor muscle tone. Babies that have a very hard spot in the middle should also be avoided. This is often a sign of yolk that has not been absorbed properly and has hardened inside the snake's digestive tract. This yolk remnant must be removed from the snake or the snake will die. Removal of the yolk can be accomplished through manual palpation, a process of gently maneuvering the yolk through the snake's system until it comes out of the cloaca. If this process is not done carefully enough, the snake can be fatally injured. The yolk can also be surgically removed. Because of the potential dangers and costs involved with treating this type of problem, it is recommended that you do not purchase a hatchling ball python that has a hard belly.

While holding the snake, take the time to look it over and check the skin carefully. It should be clean, smooth, and free from cuts, scars, and ectoparasites (mites and ticks). In cross-section the body should not be noticeably triangular in shape, with a clearly visible backbone. This is a sign of a malnourished ball python. The body should be free of sores, bumps, spinal deformities, and retained shed skin.

Check for potential respiratory problems. The nostrils should be clear, and there should be no mucus coming out of the snake's mouth or smeared on the sides of whatever container the snake was in. Avoid purchasing a ball python that is wheezing or gurgling, as these are also signs of a respiratory infection. Occasionally, a piece of skin can fail to shed out of one or both nostrils. When this happens, it may produce a slight noise when the snake breathes. Do not confuse this with a respiratory infection. The retained piece of shed is generally visible in the nostril and will most likely come out during the next shed cycle.

Parasites

Another problem to check for is ectoparasites. An ectoparasite lives on the outside of the host's body. Ectoparasites commonly found on ball pythons are ticks and mites, both of which belong to the arachnid family (which also happens to include lobsters and crabs). Ticks and mites feed by sucking blood from their hosts.

Ticks are tiny, flat, eight-legged creatures that camouflage quite well with the scales of an adult ball python until they fill up with blood and become obvious. Ticks bury their head into the snake's skin between the scales and feed on its blood. Ticks are only found on imported ball pythons or on ball pythons that have been housed with imported ball pythons. If the ball python you are looking at has a tick on it, then it almost certainly is a wild-caught snake brought in from Africa. Several years ago, ticks were fairly common

Examine a ball python's head closely before you buy it. The eyes should be clear with no shed skin stuck to them.

Herps, the Law, and You

Not enough can be said about the importance of the responsible keeping of reptiles and amphibians. Recent laws have been enacted in various states and communities across the United States that seriously limit—and in some instances even prohibit—the keeping of herps. The most commonly stated reasons for these bans and limitations are the protection of the environment or protection of the citizens. They usually come about because somebody's large pet snake, lizard, or caiman escaped recently and people are worried for the safety of children and pets.

It is your utmost responsibility as a reptile owner to ensure that your snake is being properly cared for and that you are a good example of a reptile keeper. You must make sure your ball python (or any other herps you have) cannot escape. If it does, you may become another justification for these restrictive laws. Although herpers know that ball pythons aren't dangerous to people, the uninformed and mostly snake-phobic public does not. Additionally, you should refrain from bringing your snake out to public places where people do not expect to see snakes, such as parks, community pools, and flea markets. This can startle those who are afraid of snakes and make them antagonistic toward snake keepers. If one of these people calls a local official, it could start the ball rolling toward a ban on herps.

If there is a local herpetology club, you should join and support the group. While some herpers believe that such clubs are no longer necessary, it is important to remember that these groups support conservation, serve as a valuable source of information, and work to preserve your freedom to keep reptiles and amphibians. Many of them have relationships with local law enforcement and wildlife officials, and through these relationships they are able to help formulate less restrictive laws regarding herps and herp hobbyists. Local legislators are more apt to listen to people and organizations within their communities rather than advocacy groups that come from out of the area.

Once you have had your snake for a while and know its behaviors and moods very well, consider being an ambassador for the good of herps in your local community. This is possible by first learning all the correct information you can about your snake and then going out and sharing that with others. You can start by asking at the local elementary school if a teacher or two would like to do an assembly where the children could come and learn about snakes. Perhaps this may coincide with a lesson they could be having about animals or wildlife in general. Perhaps you have children and they have a show and tell coming up at school. Contact your local Cub Scout, Boy Scout, or Girl Scout pack and find out if having you come and do a small presentation on your snake would be interesting for them. The more people you can teach about your snake or snakes, the better. If you do choose to do this, make sure that you are professional, responsible, and courteous. Also, make sure to bring some hand sanitizer along with you.

on adult ball pythons. Now, African exporters are required to remove ticks before the snakes are shipped to the United States. (Ticks are easily removed with a pair of tweezers, although care must be taken when removing a tick from the delicate tissue surrounding the area of the eye.)

Snake mites are nasty little creatures that, if left unchecked, can increase in numbers from one to hundreds in a short time. Adult female mites are black, mobile, and about the size of a pin head. These mites are egg-laying machines, and they will not hesitate to spread their progeny throughout your entire snake collection. When purchasing a ball python, carefully check around the eye sockets, the fold of skin that runs down the middle of the lower jaw, and in the labial pits. These are key areas for mite infestations. If a ball python has a serious mite problem, you will see mites crawling across your hand while you are holding the snake or after you have put it down. Avoid snakes that have mites, because they may be a vector for some diseases that are potentially fatal to ball pythons.

Transporting Your New Snake Home

Now that you have picked out a nice healthy snake, the fun part starts: bringing your new pet home! But wait! Have you set up its enclosure or cage properly? Before you even consider bringing home a ball python, you need to make sure that your cage is set up and ready for its new inhabitant (see Chapter 3). Having the cage set up before your python comes home speeds up the acclimation process.

Once you have made your purchase, take some time to inspect the bag or container that the ball python has been placed in. Make sure that it is secure, so that the snake will not escape on the way home. Ball pythons and other snakes have been lost in cars on more than one occasion when the transportation bag or container was not secure enough for the ride home. Do not place the container or bag in an area of the car where it will be in direct sunlight or under a heater vent. The ball python can seriously overheat and die within a relatively short time when exposed to temperature extremes. Stopping for a bite to eat on the way home during a warm or a cold day could also pose a threat to your new ball python. If the trip home will be a long one, bring an insulated transport container with you, one with adequate ventilation holes. This will help protect the ball python from temperature extremes. When possible, go directly home with your new snake.

Quarantining

If this is your first and only snake, then quarantine procedures will not be as important for you. However, if this is not your first and only snake, then you will need to quarantine your new arrival. All new ball pythons (and all reptiles in general) that you bring into your

A quarantine terrarium should be simple, with a newspaper or paper towel substrate.

home should be quarantined for at least 60 days and perhaps as long as 90 days. This process is a must and could possibly save you headaches in the future.

It is best—if possible—to house your new acquisition in a different room, away from your established collection. This snake should be fed last and cleaned after your other animals to avoid spreading any disease the new snake may have. Any tools or equipment that you use to work with this snake should also be thoroughly disinfected after you are done using them. Wash your hands thoroughly before and after handling your newest snake.

During quarantine, you will be able to thoroughly observe your new arrival to make sure that it eats properly, has well-formed stools, has no signs of a respiratory infection or other illness, and does not harbor mites. Following proper quarantine procedures can save you and your other reptiles a lot of trouble by preventing mites (or worse, a deadly virus) from being introduced into your collection. Once the time allotted for quarantine has passed and you are satisfied that your new snake is healthy, introduce your new arrival to its own proper place in your collection.

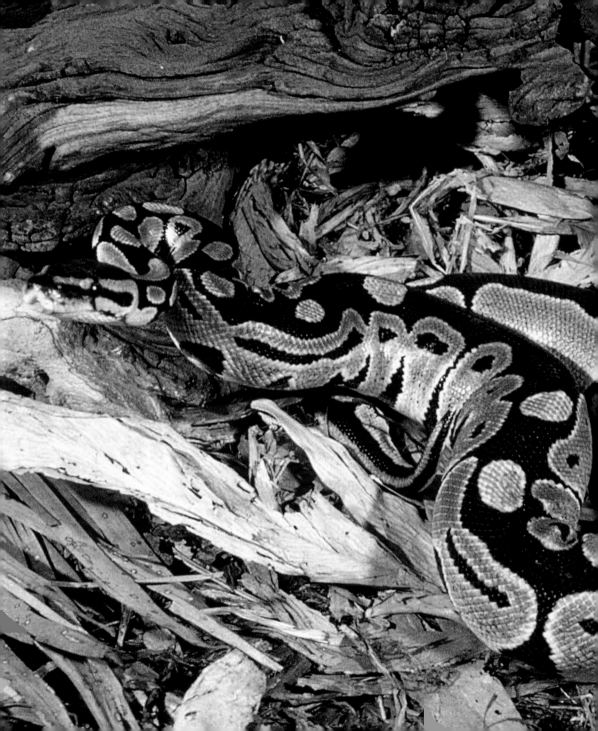

Chapter 3

Housing

Selecting the right cage or enclosure for your ball python is an important task, and some thought must go into that choice. You want the right kind of setup for both your needs and your snake's. Many different things must be considered when looking at a potential home for your future pet, some of which include the security of the cage, its size, and its insulation potential. Also, you must ask yourself if you'll be housing a single ball python or several.

A secure cage is a must-have or your ball python may escape into the outside world.

Security First

Not too long ago, the only choice available for housing reptiles were glass aquariums with homemade tops, usually weighted down with books or bricks or even secured with duct tape. This is not a secure cage. All snakes are escape artists, and ball pythons are no exception. They will find and exploit any small opening or poorly closed cage. This makes it extremely important to purchase secure housing for your snake from the very beginning.

A secure cage provides a safe environment for your snake. You want to keep the ball python in and children, guests, and household pets out. Ball pythons that are lost in a home can turn up almost anywhere. There have even been instances of home owners moving into a new home only to find that the previous occupants have left something behind—an escaped snake! Proper caging will also prevent your snake from escaping out into the neighborhood, where panic may ensue. Too many times, a loose snake has caused chaos in a neighborhood, leading to legislation unfavorable to the keeping of snakes and other reptiles.

Size Issues

Ball pythons do not get very large compared to other python species. Even so, they will require housing that is large enough to accommodate them and all of their furnishings. The number of furnishings that are placed in the cage will depend upon the type of "look" you want to achieve with your python's home. A cage the size of a 30-gallon (113.6 L) terrarium measuring 36 × 12 × 18 inches (91.4 × 30.5 × 45.7 cm) is large enough to house an adult ball python for its entire life. Be careful not to place a hatchling ball python in a very large cage. Many times, a ball python placed in an enclosure that is too large will stop feeding. If this happens, you may need to purchase a smaller cage until your python gets bigger, or else provide enough hide spots in the larger cage to help the snake feel secure.

Cage Types

When determining what type of cage you would like to use, take a few things into consideration. How many snakes do you wish to keep? How much space is available in your home for caging? What kind of caging do you prefer (functional, decorative, or a little of both)? Carefully review all of your options so that you will be better prepared to purchase the kind of cage or caging system that will work best for you and your situation.

One more thing to consider before purchasing a cage is how warm or cold the room is where you plan on keeping your snake or snakes. This is important because if you are going to keep your snakes in a fairly warm area, you may be able to keep them in glass terrariums. If your snakes will live in a basement or other fairly cool area, then you may need to look at cages that offer better insulation. Open, screened terrariums also tend not to hold humidity very well. If you live in a climate where providing heat and humidity is not a problem, such as in Florida, then a screened, glass terrarium could be a suitable choice for you.

If you do not live in such a climate, you may need to evaluate other com-

Breeders and hobbyists with large ball python collections favor rack systems for housing their snakes. They are the most space-efficient option.

You can house your ball python in a glass terrarium as long as you are able to keep the temperature and the humidity within the proper ranges.

mercially available enclosed single cages. These come in many different sizes, from a number of different manufacturers. Many of these enclosed cages come with side air vents and have heating elements placed in the side, top, or bottom of the cage, depending on the manufacturer. Custom cages are also available, and many of these are suitable for use as a piece of furniture—they can make very interesting conversation pieces in a home. If you choose to purchase one of these custom-made cages, make sure that your budget is able to handle the cost.

If you decide that you wish to keep numerous ball pythons, a rack-style system may be for you. This type of system is also be referred to as a *drawer system*. Rack systems have a supporting frame on which the cages—usually plastic tubs without lids—slide back and forth like drawers to allow for ease of cleaning and feeding. The shelf above each drawer serves as the lid, preventing the snake from escaping. These enclosures are definitely functional in nature and not very showy, but rack systems allow you to keep numerous snakes in a fairly small area. There are several manufacturers of rack-style systems. These enclosures are made out of metal or ABS plastic. The metal rack systems are much sturdier than the ABS systems, but the ABS systems offer more affordability and some offer more versatility. Rack systems can be purchased as single levels or towers; it all depends upon which type of system will fit into the space you have available.

Heating

Providing your ball python with proper temperatures is essential. Ball pythons need to be kept warm, not hot, in order for them to properly digest their food. Being either too hot or too cold may be a reason why your ball python may fail to eat or to keep its food down. You can use many different methods to keep your python's cage warm, some more suitable than others.

Hot rocks are not suitable sources of heat for ball pythons. They often burn snakes because they do not heat the air of the enclosure; to keep warm, the python must stay curled around the rock, and such prolonged contact will cause a burn.

Under-tank heaters (UTHs) are the preferred method for heating a single cage. These pads adhere to the bottom of the cage and use electricity to generate heat. Take care to avoid the possibility of creating a fire hazard in your home by reading the instructions carefully and using the heating pad accordingly. A rheostat is recommend to use in conjunction with any UTH. This device allows you to adjust the amount of heat given off by the UTH according to the temperature in your home. The bottom of the cage above the UTH should be warm, not hot, to the touch.

Ceramic heat emitters are also available for heating the cage. These are similar to light

Don't Skip the Thermostat

A temperature control system for your undertank heater is essential for the health of your ball python. A thermostat or rheostat will allow you to adjust the temperatures of the hot spot according to the needs of the snake. This will help to reduce the risk of potential injury to your snake from thermal burns. Providing proper temperatures will also decrease the risk of respiratory infection to your ball python.

Temperature Guns

Temperature guns (temperature sensors) have come down significantly in price and are now more readily available than ever. This piece of equipment will be a valuable aid in helping you maintain correct temperatures for your incubators and ball python enclosures.

Heat tape is a popular method for heating ball python enclosures.

bulbs, but they generate heat without light. They are surrounded by a metal shroud or hood that usually has a clamp on it, and you may need to build a suitable structure that will support the weight of the heat emitter and its hood. Do not use ceramic heat emitters in regular light sockets; they are likely to cause a fire. Also, care must be taken when using such a heating element. It is easy to forget that it is on and emitting heat since it does not "glow" or give off light.

Ready-made rack-style systems may come with or without heating devices and thermostats, depending on the manufacturer. Some systems use heat panels; others use heat ropes or cable. Round heat cable comes in different lengths and is relatively thin. It can be laid in loops beneath the cage floor to provide radiant heat. The amount of cable used depends upon how warm the room is: A colder room will require more heat cable underneath the cage than a warmer room.

Each cage must have a thermostat to control its heating elements. Most thermostats come with only one heat probe, but at least one commercially available thermostat comes with multiple probes. Probes are placed next to the heat source to monitor the temperature, and the thermostat is adjusted until the interior of the cage is the desired temperature. When dealing with a single-probe unit, the probe is generally best placed in the center of the cage. Units with multiple probes will allow for smaller heat gradients between the levels on a rack system. When using a single-probe system with a rack setup, the top units will always run a couple of degrees warmer than the bottom. Depending upon how many levels your rack has, a multi-probe system

No Strips

Many times, keepers put temperature strips on the outside of enclosures, thinking that these are useful and cheap thermometers. These strips do not measure the hot spot in the cage, but rather the current temperature of the glass to which they are adhered. Therefore, you should not rely on them to keep track of the temperature in your snake's enclosure.

will allow you to either heat each level individually or allow for the grouping of two to three levels at a time. This will help to reduce the temperature discrepancies between the top and bottom levels of the rack. This type of temperature difference naturally occurs in most rooms, since heat rises, and it can account for the differences in temperature between the top and bottom of the rack.

Temperature

The "hot spot" in the cage can range from 80 to 85°F (26.7 to 29.4°C) for hatchlings and 85 to 90°F (29.4 to 32.2°C) for sub-adult to adult ball pythons. The ambient air temperature does not need to be as high as the temperature of the hot spot. Ambient air temperatures can range from the high 70s to mid 80s (about 25 to 29°C).

Your snake's behavior is the most important factor in determining if the temperatures are appropriate for

Aspen bedding is one of the acceptable substrates for a ball python enclosure.

your ball python. If your snake is always in the water dish (and it does not have mites), it may be too hot. If your snake spends all of its time on the warm side of the tank and rarely ventures over to the other side, then chances are good that the cage is too cool.

Investing in a temperature gun will aid greatly in monitoring the temperature of the hot spot in the cage. Infrared temperature guns have become more readily available, and the cost is nominal. It is strongly recommend that you purchase one. The temperature should be routinely checked, as electrical equipment can malfunction, and it is important to adjust the temperature of the heating devices according to how the temperature fluctuates in your home.

A clump of damp moss inside a hide box can aid the shedding process.

Lighting

Unlike many lizards, ball pythons do not require full-spectrum lighting (lighting that closely simulates sunlight) to be happy and healthy. Their colors do look better under full-spectrum lighting, but it is not required for the health of the snake. Ball pythons do, however, benefit from a regular light cycle. In their natural range, they receive approximately 12 hours of daylight and 12 hours of night. This may vary by an hour during the dry and wet seasons. In captivity, their light cycle can correspond to the natural lengths of day and night in your area, unless you reside in the extremely high latitudes. In these regions, the amount of daylight available during the winter months may not be sufficient for your ball python, and you will need to supplement the amount of natural light that they may receive in the room. Otherwise, the natural light that comes into the room where the ball python will be housed should be sufficient.

Do not place the ball python's enclosure in direct sunlight. Placing the enclosure in direct sunlight can dramatically increase the temperature in the cage and kill your snake. If not enough natural light is coming into the room to provide your ball python with a definite day and night light cycle, supply your snake with appropriate artificial lighting that will fulfill his light requirements. This can be accomplished by using full-spectrum fluorescent lighting or any of the commercially available reptile lights.

Humidity

Ball pythons come from an area that has naturally high humidity. In captivity, maintaining the high humidity levels of the ball python's natural environment can prove quite a challenge. On the other hand, an enclosure that has humidity so high that water droplets run down the inside of the glass is too wet for a ball python. Too much moisture and your snake will get blister disease—and this is not to mention the amount of mold that will grow in the interior of the enclosure. A balance must be struck between humidity and ventilation.

Humidity levels of around 50 to 70 percent are great for ball pythons. Some ball pythons will do well with less humidity; others will require more. The type of enclosure you choose to use and the climate you live in will also determine how well the humidity can be managed in the cage. Seasonal changes will also affect the amount of humidity in your home. Winter heating lowers the level of humidity in the cage and so does the use of air conditioning in the summer. Buy a humidity gauge for the enclosure and use it to keep track of the humidity.

Proper humidity aids in the shedding process. If your snake does not have problems shedding, then you will not need to be as concerned with humidity levels. If your snake does have difficulties shedding its skin, then you may need to partially cover the top of the enclosure to increase the

Ball pythons prefer tight-fitting hide spots. Make sure the hide box you use is not too roomy.

humidity level inside. Daily misting of the cage during the ball python's shed cycle may also help to increase the amount of humidity in the cage. Sometimes this works, but sometimes daily misting can have the opposite effect: too-high humidity can also cause the snake to have difficult sheds. Once again, balance is the key, and observing how your snake behaves will aid in determining when you have achieved the right humidity for your circumstances.

Substrate

Many different types of products are available to use as a substrate or bedding for reptiles, but not all of them are suitable for a ball python. When considering which substrate to use, take into account the type of setup or "atmosphere" you are trying to create in your snake's cage.

If you are going to have a utilitarian setup, then an easily managed substrate will do. Newspaper, pre-cut cage liners, indented Kraft paper, and other similar types of paper can be used as substrate for these cages. Paper is readily available, and if you already have the newspaper delivered to your home, it can not only inform you of events, but also provide your snakes with a good, inexpensive substrate. Another benefit of paper is that you can remove it and dispose of it easily.

Shredded or chipped aspen bedding is commonly used by many hobbyists. These substrates lend themselves well to spot cleaning—just cleaning the soiled area without the need for changing out the entire substrate (although eventually the entire substrate must be changed). Aspen discolors when soiled, and this discoloration makes it easier to identify

Ball pythons can do well in a naturalistic terrarium, as long as it provides appropriate temperature, humidity, and substrate.

those areas of the substrate that need to be removed and cleaned.

Some people prefer to use indoor/outdoor carpeting or Astroturf. In the past, those were the only available options for a one-piece substrate. Now, *cage carpets* are available, made specifically for use in reptile enclosures. These pads are designed to be more absorbent and less abrasive to your pet than indoor/outdoor carpeting. If you choose to use this as a substrate, have a couple of pieces available, so that when one becomes soiled, you can quickly remove the soiled piece and replace it with a new fresh one. Make sure to clean up any fluids or fecal matter that may have seeped through the carpet onto the bottom of the enclosure.

Sand, aquarium gravel, corncob bedding, cedar wood products, and some pine wood products should be avoided. Sand can be abrasive to the belly scales of the snake, and if swallowed, can cause intestinal impaction. Aquarium gravel and corncob bedding can also cause intestinal impaction if ingested. The resins in cedar and some poor-quality pine shavings can cause respiratory distress in your ball python and should be avoided altogether.

Cage Furnishings

Hide Boxes

A hide box of some type is a must for a ball python. This will give the snake a place to rest and will provide it with the feeling of security that it needs to thrive. Numerous styles of hide boxes are available to choose from. A hide box can be as simple as a shoe box or as

Thinking Ahead

You may wish to purchase two water dishes: one for everyday use, and a larger one for times when you may be out of town for a few days. This larger bowl will provide enough water to last your ball python for the duration that you are gone.

Self-Cannibalism

Promptly remove shed skin from the enclosure once you discover it. If a shed skin is not removed from the cage before you feed your python, your snake may accidentally eat the skin if it adheres to the food item. Please be aware that although rare, this can happen. Generally, the shed skin will pass through the snake without any difficulty, but on some occasions the snake may spit the rodent out if too much shed skin gets attached to it.

elaborate as a homemade wooden house-like structure that has been properly sealed and waterproofed. You can purchase hide boxes made specifically for snakes at many pet stores.

Always keep in mind the ease of cleaning when choosing a hide box for your snake. If you do not mind scrubbing out all the intricate designs of an ornate hide box, then by all means provide your snake with one. Make sure the hide box will be large enough to shelter the ball python, but also small enough to give the snake the sense of security it needs.

Ball Pythons do not usually soak for long periods. Doing so can be a sign of mites or overheating.

If you choose to make your own hide box or to use something out of the ordinary for a hide, make sure that the opening or openings are flexible enough to accommodate the snake, both now and in the future. Ball pythons can grow quickly, and an opening that was once large enough to easily accommodate the snake may, as it gets older, become a potential death trap. You do not want to come home and find that your snake has become stuck in an opening that is too small to accommodate the middle of its body.

Many ball pythons seem to prefer hide boxes that have an opening in the top. Top-opening hides allow the snake to come out and ambush its food, without the rodent running directly into the hide.

Ceramic flower pots can be easily converted into a suitable ball python hide box. The existing hole in the bottom of the pot may require widening to properly accommodate your ball python. Once the hole has been cut to the desired size, file or sand down any rough edges that were created when the hole was enlarged so as not to leave any potential snags that may harm the snake.

Water Dish

A water dish is also essential for a ball python's cage. Choose a sturdy ceramic or plastic water dish, one that cannot be easily turned over by an adventuresome and exuberant ball python.

In general, a water dish does not need to be large enough for the ball python to soak in, but it does need to be large enough to provide an adequate amount of clean water for your pet. Many keepers use plastic food containers as "liners" for their water dishes. Water dish liners are easily removed and are simple to fill with clean water. Using a liner will help keep the water dish free from heavy mineral build-up.

Healthy ball pythons rarely soak in their water dish, and if they do, it is generally a sign of a problem. If no hide box is provided in the cage, a stressed ball python may use its water dish as a hide box. If the cage is too hot, a ball python will lie in its water dish to try to cool off.

However, mites are the number-one reason why a ball python lies in its water dish. As the mites drown, they accumulate at the bottom of the water dish. Please keep this in mind if your snake begins to spend time in its water dish. If there are no noticeable dead mites floating in the water at the bottom of the dish, however, this does not mean that your snake does not have mites. Give your snake a thorough visual inspection; if no mites turn up, double-check the temperature of the cage and make sure your snake has a suitable hide box. If this does-n't solve the problem, it's possible that your snake does indeed have mites, but they have not yet grown large enough to be easily seen.

Ball pythons will climb occasionally if given the opportunity. Be sure that any climbing branches are sturdy and stable.

Plants

Many people want to have a "naturalistic" looking vivarium, featuring plants in their snake's enclosure. You can add plants to a ball python's cage, but they will need to be very durable. Hatchling ball pythons will not do too much damage to a plant while they are small, so you may be able to use live plants in their cage. Pothos

(*Scindapsus aureus*) is a good choice. When choosing a live plant for your ball python's cage, read the label carefully. Avoid purchasing plants that are potentially toxic.

As your ball python becomes an adult, it can and most likely will destroy any live plant in its enclosure. For an adult ball python, consider using good, sturdy artificial plants. Many decorative and durable artificial plants are available, and many of these will also withstand the occasional cleaning that will be necessary when they become soiled.

Wood

Many places offer for sale decorative pieces of wood that can be used in reptile enclosures. Pieces of driftwood found on the beach may also be used, but before any wood is placed into the enclosure, it should be properly sterilized. To sterilize a piece of wood, heat it to a temperature of 135°F (57.2°C) for 30 minutes.

Any branch or piece of wood added to the cage will need to be fairly sturdy. Make sure that it does not have any notches or small spaces that your snake may become lodged in. Trying to cut a snake free from something that it has become wedged in is not an easy task. Once again,

Few snakes are more docile or easier to handle than ball pythons.

ball pythons are a fairly stout-bodied snake and anything placed in the cage will need to be able to support their weight and size as they grow. Ball pythons
are not expert climbers like arboreal snake species,
but they have been occasionally found in trees. Make
sure that the branch is securely placed in the cage to
prevent it from slipping and falling while the snake
is climbing on it.

Cleaning

Eventually, the cage will become soiled; when this
occurs, clean it as soon as possible. Some may believe
that it is not necessary to keep the cage scrupulously
clean, and while it is true that their natural habitat is
not a "sterile" environment, wild ball pythons are
also not repeatedly crawling through their own feces.
The ball python in captivity cannot choose for itself
its own environment. It has only what is provided
for it by its owner, and its living quarters need to be
kept appropriately clean. That is part of the responsibility you take on as an owner.

Skunks Without Legs

**Ball pythons, like many
other pythons, have scent
glands, and if handled
roughly or restrained too
tightly, they will "musk" you.
The musk is brown in color,
has the consistency of
mustard, and does not smell
at all pleasant. Repeated
washing of any skin that has
had this substance smeared
on it will help to reduce the
odor. It may take a couple of
days for it to be gone
completely.**

If your substrate allows for spot cleaning, spot clean areas as they become soiled. After a
couple of months of spot cleaning, it will be necessary to change out the entire substrate.
When this is done, thoroughly clean and dry the empty cage. Newspaper or cage liners generally do not allow for spot cleaning. When they become soiled, you must remove and
replace the entire piece. Make sure that you thoroughly clean the bottom of the cage before
you put in a new piece of paper or liner.

If you choose to use cage carpet, always make sure to have a second piece ready to
replace the piece that has become soiled. Having an extra package or two available will
ensure that you are prepared when the time comes to clean the cage.

Before beginning to clean the entire cage, it will be necessary to remove your snake. Make
sure you have a secure place to put your snake while you are cleaning its cage. A temporary
holding place may be a ventilated Tupperware container of appropriate size or even a pillow
case. Remember: A snake left unsecured and unattended for even a minute is a missing snake!

A mild bleach and water solution (about 1 part bleach to 10 parts water) is very effective
for disinfecting the cage. This solution can be mixed in advance and kept in a spray bottle. If
you choose to use bleach and water in a spray bottle, be sure to clearly label it to prevent it

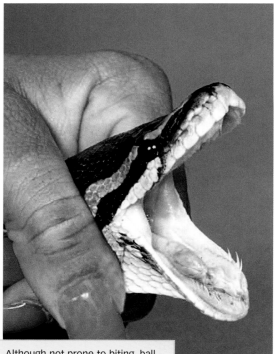
Although not prone to biting, ball pythons have sharp teeth and are fully capable of causing a careless handler some pain and bloodshed.

from being used improperly. Snakes accidentally misted down with bleach and water can die.

Remove all substrate and other material from the enclosure and thoroughly spray down the cage. After about 15 minutes, carefully wipe out and rinse the enclosure. Before placing the snake back into its cage, be sure that no damp areas are left in the cage and that all of the cleaning solution has been completely rinsed away. Some disinfectant products are designed specifically for use in herp cages. You can use one of these if you wish, but always be sure to rinse out all the residue.

If the hide box, water dish, or any decorative feature in the cage has fecal matter on it, these soiled items need to be thoroughly cleaned immediately. Soap and warm water can be used to clean cage furnishings. Once again, make sure the object has been thoroughly rinsed and dried before placing it back inside the cage.

Dirty water is a potential source for disease transmission, so the water dish will also need to be cleaned on a regular basis to prevent the accumulation of mineral deposits and the growth of algae. If you use liners, change them daily; the water dish itself will not need to be cleaned as often, but when the outside of the dish becomes soiled, clean it thoroughly.

Handling

Ball pythons can become stressed fairly quickly if they are not allowed to acclimate to their new surroundings. Allowing your new snake to settle in for a week or more is a good idea. Refrain from interacting with your new pet during this adjustment period. Once your snake has begun to feed on a regular basis, you can then begin to handle it for a few minutes each day.

Before and after handling your snake, wash your hands thoroughly with soap and warm water. Washing before handling your snake prevents you from transmitting anything harmful to your snake, and it also removes any scents from your hands that may elicit a bite from your snake. Washing after handling your snake prevents the potential transmission of any germs your snake may have to you.

Many times, when ball pythons are handled too much, they will refuse to eat. As long as your ball python continues to feed on its regular schedule, except when it is shedding, you can gradually increase the amount of time that you spend handling your snake. While handling your ball python, it is important to support the entire body of the snake and to be gentle.

Refrain from "petting" or touching your ball python's head. They do not like having their heads touched. Also, be respectful of others; not everyone may share your enthusiasm for reptiles. If your friends or family members do not like snakes, do not insist that they hold or touch your pet. Let them decide for themselves when they are ready to interact with your ball python. Do not take your snake into public areas, such as a mall or park, where there are lots of people. Many people are still deathly afraid of snakes, and as irrational as it may sound to a person who likes reptiles, those who have an exaggerated fear of snakes may, upon unexpectedly seeing your snake, have such an extreme reaction that they require immediate medical care. Taking your snake out into places like this is not in the best interest of your snake, nor in the best interest of others.

My Snake Bit Me!

Animals bite, snakes are animals, and they will bite. Will your ball python bite you? Maybe. It all depends upon you

Close-up shed ball python skin. A healthy snake usually sheds in one long piece.

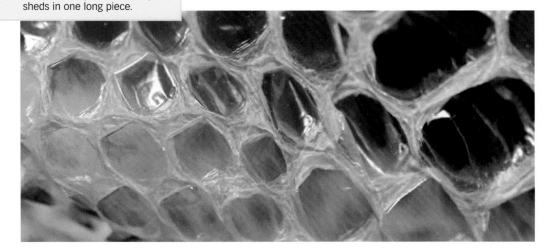

Remove shed skin from your ball python's enclosure as soon as you find it.

and your snake. Over the years, I have been bitten numerous times by ball pythons of all sizes and weights. Not one bite has ever landed me in the hospital, emergency room, or even the doctor's office. That is not to say that some of them didn't hurt—they did—but the bottom line is that the damage done by the bite is less than the damage often done by slipping and falling outside.

There are two basic types of bites, defensive bites and bites that result from feeding errors. Most bites occur during feeding and are the result of feeding errors on the part of the keeper. These are the bites that hurt—after all, the snake thinks you are food and it does not want you to get away. Often, the ball python quickly realizes that it has bitten you in error and lets go. If not, sometimes running cold water over the snake will get it to release. Using feeding tongs greatly reduces the opportunities of getting bitten, since the food item is offered off the end of tongs, not from the ends of your fingers.

Few bites are defensive. Most ball pythons cannot even be forced to bite; they really are docile and gentle snakes.

Treatment of a bite is fairly simple and straightforward. Wash the bitten area thoroughly with soap and warm water, and apply an antiseptic. Occasionally, the bite area may bruise, but this is not very common. In a couple of days, the area will be completely healed.

Escapes

"My snake got out; can you help me find it?" I get calls and e-mails like this all the time. Once again, it cannot be stressed enough how important it is to house your ball python in a secure cage. In the event that your snake does escape, be prepared to spend some time looking for it. Escaped ball pythons have been found in kitchen drawers, clothes washers, top shelves in closets, under beds, inside sofas—the list can go on and on. The general idea is that a loose snake can be found anywhere in the house.

It is very important that you do your best to find the missing serpent before someone or something else does. If it has only been a short period of time since the snake has escaped, it may be found within a 15-foot (4.6-m) radius of the cage. If it has been longer than a couple of hours, the snake could be anywhere.

Ball pythons are most active at night. Once the house has quieted down, get a flashlight out and periodically look for the culprit to be out and crawling about. There are no "snake traps" per se available to assist you in catching your snake. However, once it's dark, try placing a mouse in a small cage and put the cage an area where you think the snake may be hiding. You may find your snake trying to get into the cage to eat the mouse, or it may be waiting patiently for the mouse to come out.

It is your responsibility to do your best to find a missing snake. Sometimes, the snake may be missing for a very short time; other times, it may be gone for several months. If your home has wooden floors, sprinkle flour over the floor during the evening, and if the snake has been out roaming at night, in the morning you may find "snake tracks" in the flour that may help you to locate your missing pet.

Preventing escapes in the first place by using a secure cage will save you lots of frustration and time later. Once a ball python has found a way out of its cage, it will, once put back into the cage, continue to try to find the same way out again.

Shedding

Several times a year, your snake will need to shed its skin. Snakes shed their entire skin as they grow; they shed more frequently as rapidly growing juveniles and shed less frequently as slower growing adults.

The shedding process in ball pythons normally takes about two weeks. In the early stages of the process, a ball python's belly will commonly begin to take on a pink hue. As the process progresses, the skin will become dull and the eyes will cloud over, turning a gray or blue color. The phrase "in the blue" comes from the blue appearance of the eyes as the snake prepares to shed. After a few more days, the eyes clear up. In another few days, the

Eye Cap Removal

Before trying to remove eye caps from your snake's eye, make sure that there is actually an eye cap adhered to the eye. If you accidentally try to remove the spectacle, the clear scale covering the eye, you will permanently damage your snake's eye. If you really are in doubt about whether there is shed stuck to the eye, consult your veterinarian.

ball python begins to shed its skin. A good shed is usually defined as a shed in which all the skin has come off the snake. This can either be in one piece or in a few pieces. It is critical that all of the skin comes off. A bad shed occurs when skin is left on the ball python. This is a common sign of low humidity or possible dehydration. You will need to remove any retained skin. Allowing the snake to repeatedly crawl through a warm, damp washcloth will help remove adhered skin.

When your python sheds, carefully inspect it for retained shed. The eyes, vent, and tail tip are common areas for this problem.

Carefully check the eyes to make sure that no retained eye caps remain. Do not confuse a "cracked" or dented spectacle (the clear scale that covers the eye) with a retained eye cap. An eye that has a retained eye cap will have a slightly different appearance from the snake's other eye. On some retained eye caps, you'll notice a small piece of skin around the orbit of the eye. If your snake has a retained eye cap, use a damp cotton swab and gently rub this over the eye to remove the eye cap. You can also use a damp fingertip to carefully remove the eye cap from the eye by gently rubbing. Eye caps generally pop right off. If this does not work, you may need to take your snake to your local veterinarian to have the cap removed.

Just as retained eye caps can damage your snakes' eye, retained shed skin can damage its skin. Always check the tip of the tail for retained shed skin. This area is often overlooked, and sometimes a constricting band of shed skin builds up around the tip of the tail. When this is not corrected, the tip of the tail may die and fall off. Occasionally, skin may also remain stuck to the base of the spurs. Inspect these areas carefully after each shed. Be ready to carefully and gently remove any skin left on your snake to prevent it from causing problems.

If your ball python consistently has difficult sheds, make adjustments to the humidity in the cage; as well, you may wish to make your snake a shed box. This can be a container with a lid and a hole cut in the side that is large enough for your snake to pass through without difficulty. Make sure that all sharp edges have been filed off after you have cut the hole in the side of the container. Inside the box, place damp paper towels or damp sphagnum moss. Only use the box during the later stages of shedding, after the eyes have gone clear. Once the snake is done shedding, remove the box and thoroughly clean it out so that it will be ready to use the next time.

Records

Whether you have one ball python or 100 ball pythons, records are an important part of caring for your snake. You may ask "How can that be?" If by chance you need to take your snake into the local veterinarian's office, you will be able to show her when the snake last fed and when it last shed. You can even show the veterinarian consistent weight gain or weight loss. Records can be an invaluable tool, especially since none of us have completely perfect memories.

Information that is important to have for your records includes:
- who you purchased the snake from and when
- the age of the snake when it was purchased, or if known, the date the snake hatched
- the genetics of the snake you have purchased (if they are known)
- date of each meal the snake ate
- what it ate and how many items.
- date of each shed

Other information can be useful as well. Periodically weigh your snake and add that to your records. If your snake receives any medication, record that too. If you are going to breed your snake, write down breeding attempts and whether or not you were able to witness successful copulation. Write down the day your snake ovulates, if you are able to watch this remarkable event. Make sure you record which male you are breeding to your females. It never ceases to amaze me the number of people who hatch out baby ball pythons without being 100 percent sure which snake has fathered the clutch. This is especially important when you are using simple recessive morphs in your breeding program. Write down the day the female lays her eggs, how many eggs she laid, and how much she weighs after laying the eggs. You can even record the weight of the clutch. How detailed you wish to make your records is entirely up to you.

Records can be kept on index cards. I recommend that you keep the record card on the snake's enclosure in an inconspicuous area. If that is not possible, obtain a file box for all of your records. Some online programs also are available to assist you in your record keeping. Some are more advanced than other, and you will need to choose the one that works best for you and your situation.

Chapter 4

Feeding

ood! Few things can excite your snake more than the scent of its next meal, and few things can frustrate a keeper more than the ball python that does not get excited or even remotely interested in its food. Many factors can affect a ball python's feeding response; in this chapter, we explore some of those factors.

Like many other pet snakes, ball pythons need a diet of whole rodents. An adult ball python is capable of eating small rats.

Keepers have offered a variety of different prey to their ball pythons, including rats, mice, hamsters, gerbils, African soft-furred rats, and hatchling chicks. With the exception of mice and rats, the other listed food items have mainly been used to entice reluctantly feeding, wild-caught ball pythons to feed. Once these snakes have begun to feed regularly, keepers generally do not have much difficulty switching them over to more readily available food sources, such as mice and rats. Breeders usually offer for sale hatchling ball pythons that are already established feeders on either mice or rats.

Many ball pythons will imprint on a single food item. For example, they will recognize a mouse as a food item, but not a rat. Many ball pythons will only eat mice their entire lives. Others will only eat rats. Then there are those that will eat anything that is placed into their cage. Still others will switch between mice and rats.

Because ball pythons will often refuse one type of food in favor of another, it is best to feed your ball python what it is accustomed to eating. Be sure to clarify with the person you are buying the ball python from exactly what they have been feeding the snake and how often it has been eating. If you need your snake to feed on frozen thawed rodents, make sure you clarify that with the breeder, so that there will be no surprises when the snake arrives and you find it will only eat live prey (possibly a big problem if you live in an area where obtaining live rodents regularly is difficult). A word of caution: Do not, in an attempt to save money, feed your ball python wild-caught rats, mice, or any other small animals. Such wild-caught animals may be more aggressive in defending themselves from a predator, and they may also carry parasites that could be harmful or potentially fatal to your ball python—not to mention that this is a good way to bring fleas and ticks into your home.

Food Size

It is important to feed your ball python appropriately sized food items. Hatchling ball pythons eat large fuzzy mice (young mice that have just grown their fur) or hopper mice (slightly older and larger mice that are beginning to actively move about). They do not eat pinky mice (newborn mice that lack fur), unless they are unusually small hatchlings, such as may occur with twin snakes. If the food item offered is too small for the ball python, it may fail to elicit the appropriate feeding response. Often, when a meal is too large for a ball python, the snake will not eat it; if they are able to swallow a large food item, it may be regurgitated a day or so later. Regurgitation can lead to refusal to feed and other health issues. Avoid this problem by feeding appropriately sized prey.

An appropriate-sized food item is one that will leave a slight bulge in your snake. Adult ball pythons that eat mice will need to be offered an appropriate number of mice at their weekly feeding. The number of mice offered will vary depending upon the size of the ball python. Ball pythons 2 to 3 feet (61 to 91.4 cm)

Fuzzy mice are the appropriate size for hatchling ball pythons.

in length can be fed two mice at a feeding. Ball pythons that are 3 to 4 feet (91.4 to 121.9 cm) in length can be fed three or four mice at a feeding. These should be offered one at a time and after the previous mouse has been completely eaten. If you are feeding rats or rat pups, one should be plenty for your snake.

Live or Prekilled Food?

In many cases, a ball python that has an aggressive feeding response can be trained to eat thawed or freshly killed rodents. Whenever possible, it is best to feed your ball python dead food. Feeding dead food items not only reduces the risk of injury to your ball python from rodent bites, but it also provides for a consistent availability of food in areas where live rodents maybe very difficult to purchase on a regular basis. Rodent bites can be very dan-

No Wild Mice

Under no circumstances should you try to catch your snake's food. Feeding your ball python wild rodents puts it in danger from potential poisons that the rodents may have ingested or from parasites that the wild rodents may be carrying.

gerous and even lethal to a ball python. There have been numerous instances in which a live rodent has been left in a cage too long and has done serious and sometimes even fatal damage to a ball python. Feeding prekilled prey ensures your python will never be attacked by its food. If your ball python will only eat live rodents, do not leave the rodent in the cage for more than five minutes.

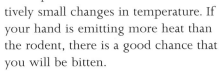
Ball pythons will often constrict prekilled prey as though it was alive.

Different stimuli are required to elicit a feeding response in a ball python: heat, movement, and scent. Keep this in mind when switching your ball python over to prekilled or thawed rodents. It is rec-

Feeding your ball python with forceps reduces your chances of being bitten. Note that pinky mice are too small to use as food for ball pythons.

ommended that you use tongs or hemostats to present the thawed or prekilled rodent to your ball python. If you choose to offer it by hand, you may be bitten. Remember, your ball python has heat pits that are able to discern relatively small changes in temperature. If your hand is emitting more heat than the rodent, there is a good chance that you will be bitten.

Rodents are easily thawed using warm water or the sun on a warm summer day. If you choose to thaw your mouse or rat out in the sun, make sure that it is not accessible to crows, ravens, dogs, or the neighborhood cat. Also, when thawing a rodent outside in the sun, check it regularly. It is amazing how quickly a rodent can begin to "cook" out in the sun.

Keep in mind that once the rodent is thawed, you should feed it to the snake immediately. This will reduce the growth of harmful bacteria. When rodents are frozen, they still contain all the contents of their stomachs and intestines. The longer they sit at room temperature, the greater the chances are that some nasty little bug will take advantage of this ideal environment and multiply rapidly. Some of these bacteria can reach such large numbers that they may cause problems for your snake. When thawing your rodent using warm water, make sure that no cold spots remain in the rodent when you pick it up. After determining that the food item has been completely thawed and is at an appropriate temperature for feeding to

Rodents: Nutritionally Complete

Since ball pythons eat the entire rodent—including bones, internal organs, and gut contents—it is not necessary to provide them with vitamin supplements. They are able to obtain all the nutrients they need from their food.

your snake, make sure that you dry the rodent thoroughly before offering it. This will reduce the amount of substrate that may adhere to the rodent's fur. Very wet fur attracts large amounts of substrate, and too much substrate attached to the rodent may discourage your snake from eating its meal.

Do not use a microwave to thaw out rodents of any size. Microwaves cook from the inside out, and snakes are not capable of digesting cooked food. There is also the possibility of the inside of the rodent being too hot and burning your snake's insides.

Feeding Frequency

You can feed ball pythons as often as once a week or as infrequently as once every two weeks. It is best not to offer food while the snake is in a shed because most ball pythons will not eat at this time. Many times, a rushed owner has placed a live food item in his ball python's cage and not checked until after a day or so, only to find that the rodent is still in the cage. At this point, the owner checks on his snake and discovers that not only is it in its shed cycle, but it has been chewed on by the rodent. Please make sure that your snake is not in a shed cycle before you offer a live rodent for feeding.

Feeding Do's and Don'ts

After your ball python has eaten, do not handle it for at least 24 hours. If you feed your snake in a separate container other than its cage, you can gently move the snake after it has finished eating its meal without causing any harm. If you handle your ball python too

Avoiding Bites

When feeding your ball python, it is best to offer the rodent at the end of a pair of 18-inch hemostats or tongs. These are used to place the food item in the cage or feeding container. Using hemostats reduces the risk of being bitten by your ball python and also reduces the risk of being bitten by an aggressive rodent. Most bites from ball pythons occur during feeding and are due to keeper error.

roughly or too soon after feeding, it may regurgitate its meal.

It is best not to disturb your ball python before you feed it. Many times, if a ball python is cleaned or handled before it is to be fed, there is a chance that it will not eat. Feeding a ball python in its cage should not be a problem; however, there are many who prefer to feed their snake in a separate container.

Once your snake has been established on a regular feeding schedule in its cage, you may—if it will help you feel more comfortable—begin to try to feed the snake in a separate container. If you choose to use a different container for feeding, make sure it is clean and secure for your snake. If your snake does not eat within a short period of time and a live rodent is left in the container with the snake, please remove it before it can injure the snake. The benefits of feeding in a separate container are that there is no substrate to stick to the rodent and that the snake will be less prone to biting (because the snake will not get used to food just dropping into its cage).

Feeding Issues

With the large number of imported ball pythons that enter the United States every year, many hobbyists buy one, take it home, and watch it refuse to eat. There may be many reasons why a ball python may not eat. It could be the time of the year: many ball pythons will fast during winter, especially wild ones used to a natural cycle of seasons. You may be handling the ball python too much: wild-caught ball pythons need time to acclimate to a captive environment. The temperatures in the cage may not be set properly: double-check your temperatures to make sure they are correct. Finally, make sure the hide box is the appropriate size for the ball python.

Once all the husbandry issues have been covered, try different types of prey items. Most imported ball pythons will eat gerbils or African soft-furred rats. If you have these prey items available in your area, offer one to your ball python, and hopefully it will eat.

If your ball python appears to be losing weight, you may need to take it to the veterinarian to be checked for parasites and possibly to start force-feeding. Force-feeding is best done

A well-fed ball python will not need to be fed while you are on vacation, but it will need sufficient drinking water.

by your local veterinarian; it should be a last resort and only done after several months of not feeding. Ball pythons can go for six months to a year without eating and only lose a small amount of weight. Rushing off to force-feed your snake after a few weeks is not in the best interest of the animal. The best way to avoid feeding difficulties is to buy a well-established, captive-bred ball python from a reputable breeder.

Vacations

A vacation is not a problem if you have other pets and have hired a pet-sitting service to take care of them for you. The sitter should be able to take care of your snake without any difficulties. All she needs to do is check that the temperature of the cage remains stable, and make sure that fresh water is always available. Your ball python will not need to be fed during this time.

If the ball python is your only pet, you can, depending upon how long you are planning on being gone, simply leave a larger-than-normal water dish in your pet's cage. By this time, you should know how long the water in your snake's water dish lasts. If you are going to be gone a week, and the dish easily holds a week's worth of water, then make sure it is topped off before you leave. If it will not hold enough water, place a spare "vacation" water dish in the cage and top it off. Barring any catastrophic event, your snake should be fine upon your return home.

Chapter 5

Health Care

Fortunately, because they do not need annual checkups or vaccinations, as other pets like dogs and cats do, it is possible to have a ball python remain healthy all of its life without ever needing a veterinarian's care.

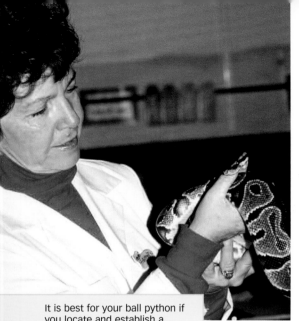

It is best for your ball python if you locate and establish a relationship with a herp veterinarian before an illness or emergency occurs.

One of the keys to keeping a ball python healthy is to begin with a well-cared-for, healthy snake. This makes selecting your ball python very important. Choosing a captive-bred ball python that has been properly maintained will give you a snake with the fewest number of health problems.

Keeping your snake healthy is your responsibility. Providing adequate temperatures in the snake's enclosure and reducing the amount of stress the snake experiences will greatly decrease the risk of your pet having problems in the future. Proper thermal gradients are necessary for the health of your ball python, along with an adequate supply of clean drinking water, a clean cage, and appropriate ventilation. Providing your ball python with its needs will reward you with a long-lived, healthy pet. Once in a while, though, something may come up that will require you to seek veterinary help for your snake. Not all of the commonly seen problems in ball pythons will result in a trip to the veterinarian; for those situations that do require veterinarian care, check with your local pet shop for good reptile veterinarian recommendations.

Finding a Herp Vet

It is not always easy to find vets who are experienced with reptiles. Here are some suggestions to help you locate a vet who can help with your ball python. It is best if you locate one before you actually have an emergency.

- **Call veterinarians listed as "exotic" or "reptile" vets in the phonebook. Ask them questions to be sure they are familiar with ball pythons.**
- **Ask at your local pet stores, animal shelters, and herpetological society to see if they can recommend someone.**
- **Contact the Association of Reptilian and Amphibian Veterinarians at their website, www.arav.org.**

Internal Parasites

If you have purchased an imported ball python, have it checked for internal parasites. Almost all imported ball pythons have parasites, whether internal or external. Common internal parasites are flagellates (single-celled organisms), nematodes (roundworms), and tapeworms. These can be detected by taking a stool sample in to the veterinarian for testing. Prior to collecting the stool sample, it will be necessary to contact your veterinarian to obtain a specimen container for the sample and to be instructed in proper collection procedures. The brown portion of the stool is the part that will need to be collected, not the white uric acid.

Testing for internal parasites is best done on at least two different occasions. Parasites or traces of them are not always shed regularly in the feces. One test may come back negative and another done a few days later may be positive. Internal parasites are treated with prescription medication obtained from your veterinarian. Follow the instructions carefully to ensure the complete removal of the internal parasites.

External Parasites

External parasites are found on the skin. In the wild, snakes can have numerous ticks attached to their bodies. In captivity, snake mites are the most common external parasite of ball pythons. Both of these types of parasites are reasonably simple to eradicate.

Ticks

At one time, it was common to find ticks on ball pythons. They can still be found on imported ball pythons, but due to better tick control in Africa, they are not as common as they once were.

Tick on the scales of a ball python (top). They can be difficult to see until they are engorged with blood. Tick shown with a penny to convey the size of the arachnid (bottom).

More on Mites

Close to 30,000 species of mites exist. Fortunately, only one type of mite is found on snakes *Ophionyssus natricis*. Mites are very species specific—this means that snake mites will not infest humans. However, it is possible to bring them home on a feeder mouse. This happens when the adult females leave a host snake to find a new one. In heavily infested pet shops, mites can hide in mice fur and hitch a ride home on them. They are not feeding on the mice, just using them as a means to find a new reptilian host.

To feed on your snake, a tick embeds its head into the skin, between the scales. You can easily remove a tick with a pair of tweezers. Grab it firmly with the tweezers just behind the head, as close to the ball python's scales as possible. Do not squeeze too hard with the tweezers; you do not wish to squash the tick until it has been removed from the snake. Gently pull back and twist the tick out of the skin. Treat the area where the tick was attached with an antibiotic ointment.

If the tick is embedded in the tissue around the eye socket, use great care in removing it. The tissue around the eye is fairly delicate, and removing a tick improperly from this area can damage your snake's eye. You may wish to coat the back of the tick with petroleum jelly; this may make it let go of the skin, and you should be able to easily remove it with tweezers and properly dispose of it. If you are unsure whether you can remove any tick from your snake without causing injury, consult your veterinarian.

Once you remove the tick from the ball python, proper disposal includes spraying the tick with an appropriate insecticide (without getting any on the snake) or dropping the tick in a small container of rubbing alcohol. If numerous ticks need to be removed from your ball python, have a container ready to collect them prior to their disposal. This container will need to be sprayed with your preferred brand of insecticide, following the manufacturer's instructions. Place the lid back on the container after each tick has been dropped inside.

Mites

Mites are a common external parasite of snakes. Think of them as snake fleas. They can be found on any species of snake, including ball pythons. Mites are smaller than ticks and move much faster. They commonly embed themselves around the eye sockets of ball pythons or under the chin in the fold of skin that runs down the middle of the bottom jaw (an area called the *mental fold* or *mental groove*).

Ball pythons suffering from heavy mite infestations will lie in their water dishes in an attempt to drown the mites. They may also look as if they have small white dots on them;

these "dots" are the mites' waste. When you hold a mite-ridden snake, the mites will be seen crawling over the snake and possibly your hand. Mites are reproductive machines, and it will not take long for one mite to turn into hundreds, even thousands. Adult females will migrate out of the enclosure looking for a new snake host.

You must permanently eliminate mites from your python and its enclosure. They are more than just an irritation; they are a hazard to your

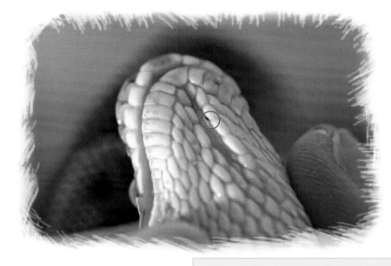

Mites (circled) often hide in the groove on the underside of a ball python's jaws, as well as in other snug places, like the vent and corners of the mouth.

snake's health. A ball python may refuse to eat if it is suffering from a large mite infestation, and small ball pythons that are severely infested with mites can die due to severe anemia. Large numbers of mites on a snake can drain it of too much blood and cause its death. Mites are easily eradicated through the use of any one of several commercially available products that are manufactured for the specific task of mite removal. Exactly follow the manufacturer's instructions for the product you choose.

Failure to Eat

One of the most common health problems with ball pythons is their failure to feed on a regular basis or at all. This is commonly seen with imported ball python adults, since they do not readily recognize a domestic rodent as a source of food. When dealing with imported ball pythons, it is best to set them up properly with a hide box, appropriate temperatures, fresh water, a quiet location, and then just leave them alone. Offer them a variety of prey items in the evening. Often, when they are ready to eat, their head will be seen at the entrance of their hide box, as they watch and wait for prey to pass by. Many times, gerbils will entice an imported ball python to eat. African soft-furred rats have also been used with great success in getting imported ball pythons to eat. Once the snake

Feeding Issues

By far the most common problems seen with ball pythons are feeding issues. Make sure you clearly understand what your snake has been eating and how it has been fed before you purchase it. If you require your snake to eat frozen-thawed rodents, make sure the seller clearly understands that is one of your requirements. Take care to provide the proper husbandry for your snake, and it should thrive and do well for you.

begins to feed regularly, switch it over to domestic rats or mice—they are much easier to obtain.

Husbandry Issues

Long-term captives and captive-bred ball pythons can also stop feeding regularly. If it is not winter—many ball pythons will fast during the winter—and your ball python refuses to feed, there may be a problem. Note that gravid females often stop eating, so rule this out first (see Chapter 5, Breeding). Stress is the greatest contributing factor to a ball python not wanting to feed. When dealing with a non-feeding ball python, trying to find solutions to encourage the snake to feed can be difficult and very frustrating.

To discover the reason why the snake is not feeding, it is best to use the process of elimination. First and foremost, double-check your husbandry. Are the temperatures appropriate for the size of the snake? Remember, hatchling ball pythons do not need to be kept as warm as adult ball pythons; they do best with hot spots of 85°F (29.4°C). Is there a hide box? Hide boxes provide a ball python with security, and most ball pythons need them. Is fresh water available for the snake to drink? There are times when ball pythons will refuse to feed if they have been without fresh water for as little as a few days, especially if you live in a dry environment. Is the ball python being kept in its own enclosure, or is it sharing its space with another ball python? Usually, ball pythons can be kept together in the same cage without any difficulties; however, many times one of the ball pythons will not eat. If this is the case, separate your snakes and set each one up properly.

Other Causes

When all husbandry issues have been checked, and if need be, corrected, and the ball python still refuses to eat, then it is necessary to examine other possible causes for your python's refusal to feed. Too much handling of a newly acquired ball python can stress the snake too much, and it will not eat. Once your ball python has begun to feed consistently, you can begin to handle your snake. Start with handling your snake only a few minutes a day. Remember not to handle your snake at all on feeding day. If your snake continues to feed regularly (except while shedding), you can gradually increase the amount of time that you spend holding your snake. This is a gradual process, and it may be necessary to take your time handling your snake so that it can become accustomed to you and your habits. If your python stops feeding, refrain from handling it until it once again starts eating regularly. At that point, you can start the acclimatizing process over again.

Is your snake going to shed? Often, when ball pythons are going into a shed cycle, they will not eat until they have successfully shed their skin. Are the seasons changing from fall to winter? Many ball python adults will fast through the winter months on into spring. This fast can be disconcerting for a first-time owner, but it does not harm the snake and it will lose very little weight during this time. A ball python that has been in my care for close to 35 years habitually goes off feed for six or seven months each year. At first, it was very distressing, but since he does it every year, I just wait until spring to begin to offer him food.

Another frequently encountered time when ball pythons may stop feeding is when heavily fed hatchlings reach weights of between 800 and 900 grams (28.2 to 31.7 oz; weights of snakes are usually given in grams because the smaller units are more accurate for these small animals). During this time, the snake will not lose too much of its weight, but it can be a very frustrating time for you as an owner, especially if you are trying to get the snake big enough to reproduce soon. They may not eat for six months or more. When this

Handling your ball python too often will cause it stress, which may in turn cause it to stop eating.

Ball Python Postraumatic Stress Disorder

It is possible for a ball python to refuse food after it has been bitten by a rat or a mouse. If this has been the case, it may take some time for the snake to regain enough confidence to resume feeding consistently. Prekilled or thawed rodents prevent this from happening.

happens, do not worry. Just be patient and periodically offer the ball python a rodent. Always offer the snake the food item it was feeding on previously. Once in a while, a ball python will change its food preference from rats to mice or vice versa. Keep this in mind when your snake refuses to feed and everything else appears to be in order.

Breeding Males

Male ball pythons must be watched carefully during the breeding season. Most of the time, male ball pythons will feed regularly during the breeding season. However, some stop feeding. You must monitor any non-feeding, breeding male carefully, or he may begin to rapidly drop weight. Without your intervention, this male will die. Remove any male that stops feeding and is losing weight from your breeding program. Set this male up in his own cage and offer a rodent that is smaller than normal. If he does not already have a hide box, place a hide box in the cage to help him feel secure. This may help him begin to feed once again.

If this snake refuses to eat after several feeding attempts, you will need to assist-feed your male python. Ask a friend to help. It is easier to assist-feed an adult when you have someone there to hold the body. For details on how to assist-feed, see the hatchling care section in Chapter 6. Gently assist-feed the male a fuzzy mouse and place him back into his cage. After a week's time, offer him another small food item. If he successfully eats it and does not regurgitate, offer him smaller food items for a month. Once he has begun to feed consistently, you can offer him his normal-sized food items. Do not breed that male again that season; you can breed him the following year if he has regained enough weight and appears healthy.

Thermal Burns

Thermal burns occur when a ball python comes into contact with a surface that is too hot or when it rests for a long period of time on a very warm surface. Thermal burns can be caused by heat lamps, hot rocks that are too hot, or undertank heaters that do not have a thermostat or rheostat attached to them.

Hot rocks are not appropriate heating elements for ball pythons. If the ambient air temperature in the enclosure is too low, the snake will never feel warm; it will wrap itself around the hot rock in an attempt to warm itself. The cool air in the enclosure will keep the snake on the hot rock as it tries to warm itself, and the cycle will keep repeating itself until the snake eventually becomes burned.

When using undertank heating pads, it is important to use a rheostat or thermostat. This allows you to adjust the amount of heat that the mat is emitting. If you use heat lamps or heat emitters to warm the cage, they must be installed in such a way as to prevent the snake from having direct contact with them.

Initially, a burn often appears as a reddened area on the belly; this is the area that usually becomes burned. Do not mistake a burn for a shed cycle. Many times, in the early stages of a shed cycle, the python's belly will take on a pinkish hue that a hobbyist could confuse with a burn. As time progresses, the burned area may begin to turn brown in color

Improper heating equipment, such as hot rocks, causes most burns seen in ball pythons.

and ooze, and the scales may begin to peel away. All but the most minor thermal burns require veterinarian care.

If your snake gets burned, change the substrate in the cage to some material that will not stick to the healing wound. Generally, paper towels or newspaper work well as a temporary substrate while your ball python heals. Your ball python will go through numerous sheds at this time as it heals the burned area. Your snake may also refuse to eat during this time. Provide the snake with plenty of fresh water, and keep an eye on it to make sure that it does not dehydrate during its recovery. Follow your veterinarian's instructions carefully while your snake is healing. Thermal burns are most easily prevented through the use of proper heating equipment.

Rodent Bites

Bites from rodents can have serious consequences for your ball python. When a live rodent is left unattended in a ball python's cage—even for a short time—it can do great damage to your snake. Mice and rats have been known to chew on ball pythons. Chew marks down the backbone and chewed tails are common. In cases such as this, it is not

The scarring on the spine of this ball python was caused by rodent bites. Feeding prekilled prey prevents this type of injury.

uncommon to see areas that have been eaten to the bone. Ball pythons with these injuries require veterinary care. Even small individual bites from rats may require a veterinarian's care, depending upon the severity of the bite. If at all possible, train your ball python to feed on thawed or freshly prekilled rodents. This will eliminate the potential problem of rodent bites.

Some bites become infected and abscessed. A veterinarian must excise these abscesses and treat the infection. In reptiles, the abscess is made up of solid material, not the more liquid material found in mammals. Since it is solid, it needs to be surgically removed from the snake.

Another thing to consider is that the toenails of mice and rats are also very sharp, and they can damage your ball python's scales. Scale damage occurs to the ball python when the mouse or rat constantly climbs over the snake as it attempts to find a way out of the cage. This type of damage may take several weeks and numerous sheds to heal. Sometimes the scales will be permanently damaged from rodent toenails.

Supervise or Feed Prekilled

The importance of supervising all live feedings cannot be stressed enough. It is true that in the wild snakes get attacked and many seem to do okay, judging by the number of imports that come in with scars. However, in captivity, scarring does not need to be a fact of life for your snake. When possible, switch your snake over to prekilled or frozen thawed food and eliminate the potential problems caused by rodent bites.

Respiratory Infections

As with people, ball pythons become more susceptible to respiratory infections when they are stressed. Stress can come in many different forms: not enough fresh water, improper temperatures, too much handling, no hide box, dirty cage, mites, breeding, new cage, and the like. Most respiratory infections become noticeable when the snake begins to wheeze. In severe cases, the ball python will sit with its head elevated, and in some instances, you will notice mucus smeared along the walls of the cage. The snake will make rather loud gurgling noises as it attempts to breathe, and mucus will ooze out of the snake's mouth.

Respiratory infections require a veterinarian's treatment; your python will need antibiotics. Make sure to have the proper tests done to determine which pathogen is causing your snake's illness. This will ensure that your snake will receive the proper antibiotic necessary to treat the infection. The temperature of the hot spot in the cage may also need to be tem-

Respiratory infections require veterinary treatment, which will normally include antibiotics.

porarily raised to help increase the snake's metabolism during treatment. This will allow the medication and the snake's own immune system to work more effectively. If your veterinarian recommends raising the heat, follow his advice. As with thermal burns, it will be essential to provide your snake with plenty of fresh water during treatment to prevent dehydration.

Regurgitation

Regurgitation is a serious issue and can be caused by a number of different things, including failure to provide adequate heat, handling the ball python too soon after feeding, feeding a meal that is too large, poor quality food item, or gastroenteritis. Gastroenteritis is a disorder of the digestive system caused by protozoa, bacteria, or poor husbandry.

When your snake regurgitates its meal, double-check temperatures to make sure they are appropriate. Check all other husbandry practices to make sure they are correct. After another day or so, offer the ball python a smaller than normal meal with a fauna replacement product (available at some pet stores and from your veterinarian). If the snake keeps down the meal, offer it another small meal in a week. Continue to feed the snake small meals for at least a month or two. If snake doesn't regurgitate these meals, all should be well. If the snake regurgitates again, a trip to the veterinarian is in order for some tests to try to determine the cause of the regurgitation. If parasites or bacteria are present that are irritating the stomach, your veterinarian will be able to prescribe appropriate medications to alleviate the problem.

If you feed your snake frozen thawed rodents and you have just recently changed suppliers, you might have received a bad batch. When a ball python eats a bad rodent, it will regurgitate it after a few days. In some cases, the snake will go through a quick shed afterward, and when the shed is complete, it will have lost some of its color. At this time, it is not known why they lose their color.

Retained Shed

Although a retained shed does not sound like a health problem, it can become one if the stuck parts of the shed are not removed. Retained sheds are a sign of low humidity or dehydration (see Chapter 2, Housing, for more information on husbandry and shedding). Several problems can arise from improper shedding. Occasionally, the shed will begin to come off perfectly and "roll" down the snake's body, but it will not roll off all the way. It will stop part way down, leaving a tight band of skin around the snake. This band can prevent the snake from eating, as well as cause decreased blood flow to areas below the constriction. This can lead to serious and sometimes fatal problems.

Tail tips that do not shed off all the way build up over time. The tip will become constricted, die, and come off due to blood loss to the area. This can also happen to the spurs. Often, the base of the spur will have layers of dead skin adhered to it that failed to properly come off. After time, these layers will eventually cause the spur to come off the snake. Skin that is adhered to the base of the spurs must be thoroughly soaked and carefully removed to prevent damage to the spur.

There may be times when your ball python will only shed in patches. You will need to remove skin that remains on the snake. If left on the snake and allowed to build up with subsequent sheds, it will cause damage to the scales underneath.

Remove patches of shed skin using a damp wash cloth or other appropriate cloth designated for the removal of retained skin. Use tepid water and allow the snake to crawl through

Hygiene, Hygiene, Hygiene

When your snake has a really bad stool or has regurgitated its meal, thoroughly clean the enclosure and perhaps even wash your snake. If your snake has feces or portions of its last meal clinging to it, clean it off. A mild dish soap can be used—be careful not get soapy water in the snake's mouth. Thoroughly rinse and dry the snake before placing it back into its clean home.

the damp cloth. The skin should come off on the cloth. Occasionally, with really stubborn skin, you may need to carefully peel it off by hand. This is best done using plenty of water. Use mildly warm water, get the snake wet, and gently rub the skin off. In some cases, you may need to rub the skin off while holding the area under running water.

Retained eye caps must also be removed. If eye caps are allowed to build up on the eye, eventually the eye will be damaged. Most eye caps are easily removed with a damp cotton swab gently rubbed over the surface of the eye. You can also use a damp finger and gently rub it over the eye. Usually, the eye cap just pops right off.

Make sure there is indeed a retained eye cap on the eye before trying to remove it. Many times, retained eye caps can be identified by noticing that the eye is a different color than the other eye. Sometimes a rim of stuck shed skin will be visible around the eye. Check for these clues before assuming that you have a stuck eye cap. A dented or creased look to the eye is not a sign of a retained eye cap. If the eye cap is stubborn and will not come off, you may need to take your snake to the veterinarian for assistance.

The best way to prevent bad sheds is to provide your ball python with adequate humidity and plenty of fresh water. This does not mean that you have to keep a very large water dish in the enclosure. A modest-sized water dish will work fine, but always make sure that there is clean water in the bowl. Fresh water in the cage will encourage the snake to remain properly hydrated, and that is the first line of defense against the bad shed.

Ball python with a retained eye cap. If this occurs, you must carefully remove the dead skin to avoid injury to the eye.

In cage setups where there is a never-ending battle to provide adequate humidity, providing your snake with a shed box may be the best solution. A discussion of shed boxes can be found in the shedding section of Chapter 3.

Diarrhea

A ball python's stool is made up of basically two parts: uric acid, which is white, and the feces, which are brown. Ball pythons do not always pass feces along with uric acid; they sometimes pass uric acid by itself. Uric acid is white and solid in a healthy ball python. A greenish color to the uric acid may indicate that your ball python is having health problems and will need to be checked by a veterinarian.

The brown portion of the stool should be well formed. A stool that is loose, runny, odoriferous, and smeared all over the cage may very well indicate that your snake has internal parasites. Improper temperature, stress, and fasting then eating a first meal may also cause loose stools, but not usually a strong, bad odor. You will need to take a stool sample into your local veterinarian's office and have it checked for internal parasites. If internal parasites are left unchecked, they can cause irreparable harm to your snake's internal organs. Follow your veterinarian's instructions carefully, and make sure your snake gets the proper treatment it needs.

Mouth rot is not common in ball pythons, but it can occur. This illness requires veterinary treatment.

Mouth Rot

Mouth rot (more properly called infectious stomatitis) is not a very common occurrence with ball pythons, but it does happen occasionally. The main causes are injury to the mouth or debris getting lodged in the mouth. Additionally, some ball pythons will strike repeatedly at objects or persons moving on the other side of a glass cage. This may occur with wild-caught adults that are very nervous and not accustomed to captivity. If the snake continues this behavior, it will eventually damage its mouth and be prone to mouth rot. Care must be taken to prevent injury to a snake's mouth. If necessary, the front of the cage may need to be covered until the snake settles in.

Once in a while, a piece of substrate will become lodged between the row of teeth and the skin of the snake's mouth. If left there, this will cause an irritation in the mouth, and it can become a real health issue. If you house your snake on a substrate other than paper,

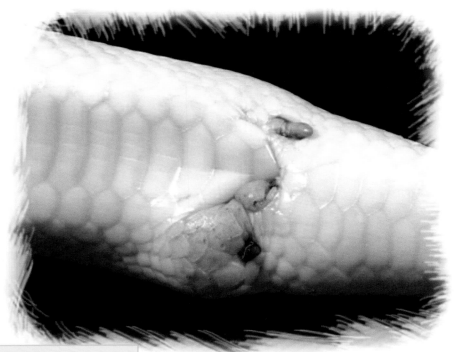

Infected hemipene caused by overbreeding. If you are going to breed your ball pythons, make sure you have enough males for your females.

make sure its mouth is clear after it has eaten to prevent problems that can occur from debris becoming lodged in its mouth.

Mouth rot can cause the loss of teeth, and in severe cases, even the destruction of the bones in the jaw. If you suspect your snake has mouth rot, a trip to the veterinarian is in order. The earliest signs of mouth rot are a bright red spot or spots on the gums, excessive salivation, and yellowish, cheesy material in the mouth. A ball python suffering from mouth rot may refuse food because it will be painful to eat.

Infected Hemipene

Infected hemipenes occur primarily in two different ways: overuse of the organ and the accidental withdrawal of foreign material into the body. The hemipene is designed to fold back into the cavity in the male's tail. This action generally cleans off any debris that may be stuck to the hemipene upon withdrawal from the female. Once in a while, the system does not work properly and a piece of substrate will end up in the body cavity along with the hemipene. This can cause an infection of the area. One way to avoid this problem is to breed your snakes on paper.

Overuse of the organ is just what it sounds like—just because a male can breed a dozen females doesn't mean he should. Many breeders try to stretch their males out as far as possible without realizing the potential damage that can be done. They do this so that they only need to purchase and maintain the smallest number of males possible. When a male has been too busy breeding, the area around the cloaca will develop what appears to be herniated tissue. In severe cases, the area will be so malformed that the hemipene will not be able to be used at all. This requires surgery, and not all veterinarians are capable of preserving the hemipene. Many will just remove it. Surgery to remove the herniated tissues and/or infected tissue around the cloaca and any abnormal tissues from around the hemipene will be very costly. This extra expense is something to keep in mind when you are setting your males and females up for the breeding season. For information on the proper number of males in a breeding program, see Chapter 6.

Miscellaneous Issues

Many possible misadventures can happen to your ball python, and some are more likely to happen than others. Here are a few possible health problems ball pythons can acquire, but they are not common occurrences.

Prolapse

A prolapse occurs when tissue that is supposed to be inside the body ends up on the outside of the body. Cloacal prolapses and hemipenal prolapses can occur. Both require immediate attention. The tissue that has prolapsed must be kept clean and moist. Unless you have had years of experience dealing with snakes and their various problems, the best course of action is to take your snake to the veterinarian as soon as possible for immediate treatment—this is an emergency situation!

Spinal Injuries

Occasionally, an unfortunate accident will

Quarantine

Depending upon how many animals you are keeping, you may need to set up a quarantine area for your snake based upon what is wrong with it. Respiratory infections, diarrhea, regurgitation for unknown reasons, and mites are all circumstances that warrant the affected snake to be placed in quarantine. You can find details on quarantining ball pythons in Chapter 2.

Wash your hands before and after handling your snake to prevent transmission of bacteria between the two of you.

happen to a ball python; it may be dropped on a cement floor or accidentally shut in the door or lid of its enclosure. Ball pythons are remarkable resilient, and it is amazing the things that they can live through. However, if the injury is severe enough to cause partial paralysis of the snake, the humane thing to do is to have it euthanized by a veterinarian. Sometimes the injury will heal and the snake will only have a slight deformity. As long as it does not affect the passage of food or waste through the body, the snake should be fine. Once in a while, though, the spine will continue to contract and the ball python will develop numerous kinks down the spine. If this begins to happen then, once again, you will need to make a decision on what would be the best course of action for your snake.

Retained Eggs

Out of the hundreds of clutches of eggs we have had laid at our facility during the past 15 years, we have only ever had two females that have had problems with retained eggs. If you believe that your snake has retained an egg after she has laid her clutch, you will need to take her to the veterinarian to have the egg aspirated and/or removed from the female surgically.

Rubbed Noses

Once in a while, you will find a ball python that will rub its nose or push on a corner of the cage to the point at which an infection will begin under the skin. Your veterinarian will need to surgically remove the infection. We have also had instances when hatchling ball pythons have found a rough spot in their cage, usually around an air hole. They actually pushed so much on that particular spot that they completely rubbed away a portion of their rostral scale. It is very important to make sure that there are no rough spots in your ball python's enclosure.

Salmonella

Salmonella is a really hot topic for reptile enthusiasts, as well as for those who do not wish for us to be able to keep reptiles. Those who are against us having reptiles and amphibians as pets exaggerate the dangers of keeping these animals. I have been asked many times if a person's ball python will make him sick. My response is that you are more likely to catch salmonella from the food that you eat than you are from your pet snake. My family and I have never caught salmonella from our reptiles, and we have had them with our family for 20 years.

However, it is certainly possible to contract salmonella from a reptile. As with any animal you own, you must practice proper hygiene. Always wash your hands with warm water and soap after you have handled your snake or cleaned its cage. Do not allow your snake to crawl across countertops where you prepare food. Do not allow your snake to crawl across the table where you eat your meals. Do not eat, drink, or smoke while handling your snake. If you allow your snake to swim in your bath tub, thoroughly clean the tub before you use it. When friends or family handle your snake, make sure they thoroughly wash their hands with soap and warm water, before and after they pick up your pet. Be especially careful with younger children; they often place their hands in their mouths without warning. Do your part to ensure that you and your family will not become a negative statistic in regards to reptiles and salmonella.

Chapter 6

Breeding

Breeding your ball python opens up an entire new world of experiences and challenges—from a successful breeding to the excitement of your first clutch of eggs and then on to seeing the noses of hatchlings poke up out of their eggs! It is always fun, every year, to watch new babies come out of their eggs and to marvel at their colors and patterns. I hope you will have as much fun hatching your own ball pythons as we have had.

Sexing

Before embarking upon your breeding trials, you will first need to determine the sex of your ball pythons. Ball pythons, unlike some other boas and pythons, cannot be accurately sexed based on their spur size. Both males and females have cloacal spurs, and they can be very long and thin or short and thick regardless of the sex of the ball python. These spurs are found on either side of the cloaca or vent. Spurs do wear down on adult males and can even come off due to an excess of retained shed skin built up around the base of the spur. Spurs can also be lost due to vigorous spurring of the female.

Adult ball pythons are generally sexed by probing. A steel probe is inserted into the base of the tail. Male ball pythons will probe, on average, to a depth of eight to ten subcaudal scales (the scales on the underside of the tail posterior to the cloaca).

Although males tend to have longer spurs than females, this is not a reliable method of sexing. Here is a female with one long spur and one broken one.

The most accurate way to sex ball pythons is by probing. Have an experienced person show you how to perform this delicate procedure.

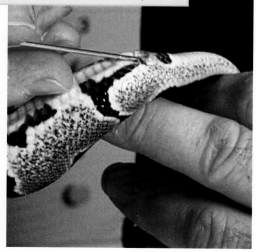

Females, on average, will probe to a depth of four subcaudal scales. Please remember that this is a general guideline—some specimens will not probe to the depths indicated. Some females have probed to a depth of seven subcaudal scales and some males have probed out at four.

If you have purchased snakes of unknown sex, your local veterinarian should be able to sex your snakes for you. Most breeders will sell you snakes that have already been properly identified as male or female.

Hatchling ball pythons are commonly sexed by manually everting the hemipenes; this procedure is referred to as "popping." It involves putting gentle pressure on the tail just behind the cloaca and watching to see if hemipenes pop out. Only experienced people should try this because it is easy to injure snakes when everting their hemipenes.

Conditioning

Once the gender of your snakes has been determined, you will need to condition them for breeding. First-time breeding males do best when they weigh around 700 grams or about 1.5 pounds. It may take a male a year and a half to reach this size. First-time females should weigh 1,500 grams or about 3 pounds. It may take a female three years to reach this size. As females and males mature, they will naturally get longer. Longer females will need to weigh more than 1,500 grams to produce good fertile clutches. There is a definite length-to-weight ratio for female ball pythons. A female that is 4 feet (3.5 meters) long must weigh more than 1,500 grams to produce a viable clutch of eggs. She will more than likely need to weigh closer to 2,200 grams or about 4.5 pounds. The ability of any given female to success-fully produce viable eggs is directly linked to the amount of fat she has stored. Too much or too little fat inhibits the ability of the follicles to properly develop.

Once your snakes are the appropriate size and age, you can begin to consider breeding them. In captivity, ball pythons are considered nonseasonal breeders. This means that they can be bred during any time of the year. However, most breeders tend to breed their ball pythons during the winter, when day lengths are shorter and the ambient air temperatures are cooler. Do not place your ball pythons in hibernation, as this process will kill them. They only require a slight cooling during the breeding season. It is best to cool your ball pythons for about a month prior to introducing them to each other. During this time, the ambient air temperature during the day can be in the mid 70s (about 23°C to 25°C) and drop down to the low 70s to high 60s (about 20°C to 22.5°C) at night. The snakes will still need a hot spot during this time. Daytime highs at the hot spot can be 90°F (32.2°C), with nighttime lows of 80°F (26.7°C).

Watch your snakes' behavior. If they are always on the cool side of the cage, turn down the heat a little. How your snakes behave will give you important clues as to how to develop an

Leave It to the Experts

Your snakes must have their sex determined by someone who has experience with this procedure. If you try to determine their sex on your own without proper training or equipment, you could injure your snakes or get inaccurate results.

Ball Pythons Don't Hibernate

Do not hibernate your ball pythons. Their natural range does not get that cold, and they are not designed to withstand cold temperatures. Some cooling has been found to be essential to stimulate the reproductive activity of these pythons, but never cool them as you would a temperate-dwelling snake, such as a corn snake.

effective breeding program. Breeding season can begin as early as September and go through May. Normally, ball pythons are bred in October through March in the northern hemisphere. For the southern hemisphere, the breeding season corresponds to the months of May through October.

Breeding Attempts

For breeding attempts, males can be introduced into the female's cage or vice versa. It does not matter how the snakes are introduced, as long as the process you choose works for you and your snakes. During the breeding season, it may be best to breed your ball pythons on a paper product, such as newspaper, cage liners, or indented Kraft paper. Occasionally, a male may take in a piece of substrate when he retracts his hemipene. A paper substrate will reduce the risk of a foreign body being taken into the area where the hemipene is retracted. Such foreign objects can cause inflammation of the hemipene and can lead to an infection.

Courtship and Mating

One male can be used to breed up to five females. It is possible for them to breed more than five, but five is a realistic number to work with. Ball pythons will copulate for as long as 24 hours. Before copulation occurs, the male will court the female. He will often climb up on the female and begin to rub her with the lower third of his body. He will also rub the female with his spurs.

A receptive female will raise her tail or allow the male to raise her tail and attempt

Only breed ball pythons that are in perfect health with good weight. This caramel albino appears to be a good candidate for breeding.

copulation. Receptive females, whose follicles are beginning to develop, give off the appropriate pheromones that attract males and stimulate courtship. The raising of the tail precedes copulation. Copulation occurs while the tails of the two snakes are entwined. If the female is not interested, she will vigorously wag her tail and may even throw the male off when he attempts to copulate. When the female behaves in this manner, it is not the right time for her to breed, and you will need to separate the pair and try again in a few weeks.

Once copulation is complete, separate the snakes. The pair can be placed back together several times during the breeding season to ensure that at least one breeding was successful. Even though a male can breed numerous females, it may not always be advisable to stretch a male out to the maximum number of females that he can handle. Males that have been "overbred" can develop infections of the hemipene and surrounding tissue. Surgery is not always necessary, but there are times when it will be necessary to remove the infection from the tissue, and this is not an inexpensive surgery. Keep an eye on your male and remember, just because he can breed many females, doesn't mean he should.

Mating between an albino and a spider ball python.

Feeding During Breeding

Even though ball pythons experience cooler temperatures during the breeding season, they can still be fed on a regular basis. The size of the food item needs to be smaller due to the decrease in temperature. During this time, it is very important to keep an eye on your breeding male. Males can drop weight fairly quickly during the breeding season, and there have been instances where small males have bred themselves to death. Larger males may also develop difficulties; some drop too much weight and begin a downward spiral, refusing to eat and developing loose runny stools. Failure to quickly realize that your male is having a problem may result in his untimely demise. Males that begin this type of downward spiral need immediate attention. Remove them from your breeding program and offer them food. If they continue to refuse to eat after a few attempts, you may need to assist-feed them a small food item such as a fuzzy mouse. See Chapter 5 for a more thorough discussion of this problem.

Monitor the weight of your male carefully. A lot of emphasis is placed on the female and the amount of weight she needs to develop her follicles, but breeding also takes a toll on the male. Make sure your male is in good shape for the upcoming season. Males that have had difficulties during breeding season may take up to a year to fully recover.

Ball pythons lay six eggs per clutch on average, but the number varies greatly.

Ball Pythons

Fertilization and Gestation

A female generally has follicles (ova or immature eggs) present throughout the year, but they are fairly small. Body weight, temperature, and other environmental factors cue the growth and development of the follicles inside of the female. Females can develop large follicles without ever being introduced to a male. However, these follicles will be reabsorbed if the female is not introduced to a male in a timely manner and if successful copulation does not ensue. Reabsorption of follicles is a fairly long process, and it can take several months for the follicles to be completely reabsorbed.

Like other pythons, female ball pythons coil around their clutches and incubate them.

When copulation is successful, a female's follicles will continue to develop. Once a female's follicles have developed past a certain size, she will refuse to eat. During this time, it is important to make sure that the female has the appropriate temperatures for proper development of her follicles. Females can "hold" their follicles until circumstances are right for her to ovulate. The difference of one degree in temperature can be all that is needed to encourage ovulation.

Sperm can be held in the female for several months before fertilization takes place. Fertilization occurs during the process of ovulation. Ovulation is the release of the ova from the ovarian follicle. The released ova then move to the oviducts. Ovulation does not last for a long period of time—usually only a day—and you can easily miss it. When a female ovulates, the lower third of her body becomes distended, making her look as if she has just eaten a very large meal. Some females have very noticeable ovulations, while others may not be as obvious. If you are able to catch a female ovulating, it is a very interesting process to watch. You can actually watch the female as she undulates portions of her body to move the ovulated follicles into the oviduct.

The eggs become shelled after ovulation and fertilization. Once the follicles are shelled, they can no longer be reabsorbed. Once the female has ovulated, she will no longer need to be bred by the male. After ovulation occurs, the female will begin to seek out the warmer areas of her enclosure. She may also be found lying upside down or in odd positions in her cage as she thermoregulates. About three weeks after ovulation, the female will go through her pre-egg laying shed. Once in a great while however, the occasional female will not have a pre-egg shed. This is the exception, though, not the rule. After the pre-egg laying shed, the female generally will lay her eggs in an average of 30 days. If she is kept too cool, it will be longer, and if she is fairly warm, the time may be shorter.

Nesting

All snakes are individuals, and ball pythons have their share of individuality. Some females will not need a nest box, while others will cruise their cage continuously looking for a suitable place to lay their eggs. For these females, you should provide a nesting box. The box must fit into the female's enclosure and should be easily accessible to her and you. Place damp sphagnum moss inside the box. Make sure to keep an eye on the moss so that it does not dry out or mold. The moss should be damp, not wet.

Ball python clutch incubating on vermiculite. These eggs are starting collapse, indicating they are either near hatching or being kept too dry.

The process of egg laying takes several hours. Often, the female will begin to lay her eggs some time in the late evening or early morning. Commonly, the female is found in the morning, coiled nicely around her clutch of eggs, or she may just be finishing laying her clutch. Upon occasion, a female will lay her eggs during the day. This is the exception, but you never know when you will be the one experiencing the exception. It is always best to check females that are expected to lay in the morning and in the evening. If the female is discovered in the process of laying her eggs, it is best to let her finish with minimal disturbance. Female ball pythons during and after egg laying can be fairly aggressive.

Occasionally, a female will only lay one egg and the remainder of the clutch will follow several days or even a week later. This does not happen very often, but when it does, the egg laid before the rest of the clutch always fails to incubate to full term.

Mom Knows Best

Female ball pythons have been known to occasionally kick out an egg or two from their clutches. She may be coiled around all of her eggs but one. Invariably, the kicked out egg also fails to hatch. It seems as if some females already know which eggs will not remain viable, and they will not include them with the group. When the nonviable egg begins to decay, it is not in contact with the rest of the clutch. This reduces the risk of exposure to potential molds that may destroy the remainder of the clutch.

Incubation

Before the arrival of the eggs, you must decide whether to artificially incubate the eggs or allow the female to maternally incubate them. Maternal incubation will work as long as the female is a good mother and has the right environment in her enclosure. She will need to be left undisturbed and kept at appropriate temperatures and humidity: 88 to 89°F (31.1 to 31.7°C) and near 100 percent humidity.

Female ball pythons that are good mothers will remain coiled around their eggs until they begin to hatch. The female will loosen and tighten her coils depending upon how warm or cold the eggs are. The female must have access to clean drinking water during this time. Placing the water bowl within easy reach of the female will be helpful to her. Female ball pythons have been observed leaving their eggs to get a drink of water, then returning to their eggs when they have satisfied their thirst. The male, if he is housed with the female, needs to be moved into his own cage. Females that are allowed to incubate their own eggs will not feed during this time, and they may take longer to regain their weight compared with females whose eggs have been artificially incubated.

When using an incubator, set it up and make sure it is stabilized a week or two before the eggs are due to be laid. Place it in the most temperature-stable room in the home or facility. There are many different commercially available incubators on the market today. Make sure to do your research into which one will work the best for your budget and the number of clutches you wish to incubate.

Do not place the incubator temperature control probe inside the egg container. The temperature inside this container will increase as the eggs approach the time when they are due to hatch—sometimes by several degrees. If the probe is inside this container, it will register this change in temperature and cause the incubator to be too cool.

The Egg Container

Place the egg-holding container in the incubator during the time it is stabilizing. This will allow the contents of the container to reach the appropriate temperature and will also allow for adjustments to be made to the size of the container in case it is too large for the incubator. The container should have a lid that allows for easy viewing of the eggs while they are incubating.

The egg container will need a substrate (usually called the *incubation media*) inside for the eggs to rest on. The mixture used for incubating ball python eggs can be perlite or a mixture of perlite and vermiculite. You can find both of these materials at gardening supply stores. If you decide to use both perlite and vermiculite, make sure the vermiculite mixture has no other additives in it as these may cause the eggs to mold. When using vermiculite and perlite, they can be mixed together using one part perlite and two parts vermiculite by volume. Add water to the mixture to keep the eggs at the proper humidity. It is important not to get the mixture too wet; if it is too wet, the eggs may mold and perish. One part water for every five parts of dry mixture by volume is a good starting point. Adjustments may need to be made to the amount of water that needs to be added to the mixture, depending upon the climate where you reside. Generally, ball python eggs begin to collapse

Be Prepared

Before your eggs arrive, make sure that you have your incubator already set up and stabilized. Make sure you have placed the incubator in the most temperature-consistent room in the house.

two weeks prior to hatching, as long as the incubation mixture holds the appropriate amount of moisture. If the mixture is too dry, the eggs will begin to collapse much earlier during the incubation process. It is not necessary to remove the eggs when adding more water to the mixture. Just carefully pour in small amounts of water into the substrate around the eggs. The mixture is important, because it supports the eggs and holds the amount of moisture necessary for them to survive until hatching.

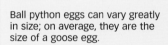

Ball python eggs can vary greatly in size; on average, they are the size of a goose egg.

Moving the Eggs

Removing the eggs from the female can be tricky business. Female ball pythons are often protective of their clutch. Some will defend themselves and their eggs quite vigorously. Before taking the female off her eggs, make sure she has completed the process of laying her entire clutch. When you have determined that she is finished, have a container or pillowcase ready to place her into once you have removed her from her clutch. Occasionally, a small towel may be placed over the female to help calm her down.

Here is a moldy egg leaking fluid. The other eggs have not been affected by the bad egg, which should be removed from the incubator.

You may need to uncoil her tail first and carefully remove her from the eggs. Try not to let her cling to the eggs too much. Once she has been successfully removed from the clutch, place her in the container or pillowcase to keep her safe until the clutch has been dealt with.

Take care when moving the eggs. Often, the eggs will be adhered together in a clump. It is important to not drop eggs, or to let any of the eggs roll around when moving them. If the eggs are in a clump, just place them in the container that way. It is not necessary to separate them. If you feel you must separate the eggs, or if it is necessary to separate them so that they will fit into the egg container, use dental floss to gently tease apart the eggs. Separating the eggs is easiest when it is done fairly soon after the female has finished laying them. At this time, they are not as strongly adhered to one another as they will be in a few more hours.

About the Eggs

Fertile eggs are white in color and are about the size of a goose egg. Ball python eggs are not hard-shelled like a birds' egg, but instead are slightly pliant and leathery feeling to the touch. When candled (the process of holding a small bright light such as a penlight up to the side of the egg), a well-defined vein system along with an embryo can be seen in the egg. Ball pythons begin developing after fertilization so that, by the time the egg is laid, the embryo is already well on its way to becoming a baby snake. I recommend that you candle all of your eggs before placing them into the incubator. Most flashlights will do the trick. Candling works best in a room that is not brightly lit. If possible, take the clutch into a darker room and carefully candle them. Eggs that do not contain embryos need to be discarded.

When kept between 88 and 89°F (31.1 and 31.7°C), ball python eggs will hatch in about 60 days.

Twins hatching out of the same egg, a rare event. Twins are smaller than normal hatchlings and may need smaller food.

If you are lucky enough to catch your female laying her eggs, the embryo will be clearly visible until the shell dries. Occasionally, it is possible for a ball python to lay an egg that appears to be viable—it has the right color and size—but has no embryo present. This is an infertile egg. These eggs usually will collapse and become moldy within two weeks of being placed into the incubator. *Slugs* or ova that failed to develop are much smaller than fertile eggs. They are of a different color and texture and can be disposed of immediately.

Occasionally, an egg will have one end that did not calcify properly. This end will be a gold brown in color, and the egg may have the shape of a teardrop. These eggs can be incubated with the rest of the clutch as long as there is an embryo present within the egg. When I set these types of eggs up in the incubation substrate, I make sure that the end that is not properly calcified is above the incubation medium and not resting in it. The hatchlings that come from these types of eggs will almost always be much smaller than their siblings and will need to be fed correspondingly smaller food items. The surface of other eggs in some clutches may appear to be unevenly calcified. As incubation proceeds, these eggs may begin

Staying Put

Once in a while, a hatchling will remain in the egg much longer than the rest of clutch. If the yolk has been fully absorbed, this hatchling will need to be manually removed from the egg. For some unknown reason, there are those hatchlings that just insist upon staying in the egg. At other times, a hatchling may not leave the egg due to skeletal deformities. Deformed baby ball pythons should be humanly euthanized.

Carefully pick up the egg and inspect the hatchling; if the yolk has been absorbed, but the snake does not wish to come out, very gently remove the snake from the egg. It will be necessary to rinse the "goo" off the hatchling before placing it into its cage.

to look as if they have dimples all over them. Just maintain proper humidity and temperature, and they should hatch with no problem.

Once in a while, an egg or two may have a small or large brown spot on the surface. These are often referred to as *windows*, and if you have one that is large enough, you may be able to see the developing snake inside of the egg. If the egg clump has been left intact and an egg begins to mold in the center, do not worry too much. If the mold concerns you, use cotton swabs to carefully wipe the mold away from the edges of the other eggs. If the eggs are set out individually in the box, and an egg begins to mold and collapse, you can discard that egg. Eggs that begin to get green or blue "water marks" on them are no longer viable and should be removed. Eggs that have died also begin to smell. This is a really great way to determine for certain that the egg is no longer viable.

Temperature and Humidity

While the eggs are incubating, it is important that the temperature remain fairly constant. Since the incubator has been running for a couple of weeks before the eggs arrived, this should be a fairly simple task. The quality of the incubator will also determine how stable the temperature will remain.

Ball python eggs incubate best between 88 and 89°F (31.1 and 31.7°C) with close to 100 percent humidity. At these temperatures, the eggs will take approximately 60 days to hatch. You will need to vent the container every so often to prevent the air inside the egg container from becoming stale.

When ball python eggs are incubated at too high above their optimum temperature, skeletal deformities of the developing ball python can and do occur. Temperatures that are too low often result in fully formed hatchlings that are dead in the egg. The humidity should also be watched closely. If the eggs begin to collapse soon after placing them in the incubator, the incubation substrate may be too dry, and a small amount of water will need to be carefully added. It is possible to kill the eggs through dehydration and the opposite is also true—it is possible to kill the eggs by using too much water. Make sure to label the incubation container with the expected hatch date of the clutch. When the eggs begin to collapse, having this date readily available on the container will allow you to determine if the eggs are collapsing too early.

Hatching

Approximately two weeks prior to hatching, the eggs will begin to collapse. This is a normal process and should not give you cause to worry. Water droplets will also begin to condense on the top of the egg container as hatching approaches. This is also natural and should not cause concern. The condensation occurs due to the temperature difference between the inside of the egg container and the interior of the incubator. The temperature inside of the egg container has increased due to the activity of the developing snakes.

The eggs should begin to pip (the slicing of the egg shell by the hatchling) around day 60, as long as the temperature has remained fairly constant at 89°F (31.7°C). The hatchling snake usually will make several slits in the egg before it will find one to its liking and poke its nose out.

Hatchling albino ball python. Set up each hatchling in its own enclosure to avoid feeding problems.

Within a day or two, the entire clutch of eggs should be slit. Baby ball pythons will sit inside the egg for at least a day before they will crawl out. Do not disturb them during this time. They are in the process of absorbing any remaining yolk that has not been used during their development in the egg. The absorption of the yolk is an important process that will provide the hatchling with nutrients that will sustain it until it eats its first meal. When the yolk has been fully absorbed, the area where it was attached to the snake, the umbilicus, will have properly sealed.

Hatchling Care

Hatchling ball pythons must be housed in their own separate cages. Failure to house them separately may result in some or all of them refusing to feed. There have also been rare instances of cannibalism among hatchling ball pythons. They will need to be provided with a hot spot that runs between 80 and 85°F (26.7 and 29.4°C) and with a water dish. In about 10 days, they will have their first shed and can be offered their first meal, a fuzzy mouse. If you have access to pinky rats, these may also be tried. Once in a while, there will be a stubborn hatchling that will not eat. Provide this one with a hide box and try offering it a slightly smaller or different food item. If all efforts fail and it has been a couple of weeks, it may become necessary for you to assist-feed this hatchling.

Assist-feeding is not force-feeding. It is done with a smaller food item than what the hatchling would normally eat. The rodent is euthanized and gently pressed against the nose of the ball python where the tongue comes out. Once the hatchling has opened its mouth, carefully place the nose of the rodent in the back of the snake's mouth as far as you can. Carefully close the jaws of the hatchling over the rodent and carefully put the snake down. Try not to disturb the hatchling. Nine times out of ten, the baby ball python will eat the food item. Gently pick it up and place it back into its cage. When feeding day comes around next, offer the baby ball python its usual fare; if the snake refuses, you may assist-feed it again. Usually, you will not need to assist-feed a ball python hatchling more than a few

Wiggle It

When offering frozen thawed rodents to your hatchling ball python, make sure you offer them off a pair of tongs or hemostats. Sometimes just laying the thawed rodent in the bottom of the cage is not enough to elicit a feeding response. The hatchling might want moving food!

Breeders produce an astonishing variety of ball pythons by crossing different morphs. This is a pastel spider.

times before it will begin to readily eat on its own.

Different stimuli are required to elicit a feeding response in a ball python: heat, movement, and scent. Keep this in mind when switching your ball python over to pre-killed or thawed rodents. Once the hatchling has developed or demonstrated an aggressive feeding response, it is time to switch it over to pre-killed or thawed rodents. Using a pair of 18-inch (45.7-cm) hemostats, present the dead food item to the hatchling ball python. You may have to "wiggle" the food some to simulate movement. If you are using thawed rodents, make sure the food is completely thawed and warm enough to elicit a feeding response. Generally a "warm enough" thawed rodent is one that feels warm to your touch, not hot. Often, if the thawed rodent is too cold or too hot the ball python will not recognize it as an acceptable food item and no feeding response will be seen.

Chapter 7

Ball Python Genetics and Morphs

Remember back in high school biology when you were studying genetics using pea plants to determine what colors their flowers could be? Did your eyes glaze over? Did you ever think that you would use any type of genetics in your life? Well, now is your opportunity to return to those days and brush the cobwebs out of your mind. Genetics is not the easiest subject, but it is essential to understand the basics as you pursue your quest to produce unique ball pythons.

Basic Genetics

Before taking a look at the many different color and pattern mutations that are available in the ball python market today, it is important to have a basic understanding of genetics. This knowledge is essential when planning your breeding projects, and will help protect you from sellers who are trying to take advantage of people who do not understand how the various color and pattern mutations, also known as morphs, are produced.

Some of the basic genetic terms are listed here.

DNA: Deoxyribonucleic acid. This is the molecule that forms the genetic code.

Chromosome: Most cells in living organisms have a nucleus. Much of the nucleus is made up of paired chromosomes; the number of pairs is constant within a species. Each chromosome is a single, long strand of DNA in a protein matrix.

Albino ball python. This is a simple recessive mutation.

Gene: The units of DNA that are transmitted from one generation to the next in the sperm and egg cells. Each gene codes for a specific protein. Each protein functions in a specific step in the biochemical pathway that determines an individual's phenotype. There are numerous genes on each chromosome.

Allele: One of two or more alternate forms that a gene may take. A changed, or mutant, allele at one locus can block or divert a biochemical pathway to produce a phenotype that is different from the normal.

Locus (plural = loci): The location on a chromosome where a specific gene resides. Think of it as a street address.

Genotype: The genetic makeup of a plant or animal. The identity of an allele or alleles that a single individual has at one or more specified loci.

Phenotype: The physical characteristics (such as eye color or scale color, but also including physical traits not easily observed, such as innate disease immunity) of the animal as dictated by the genes it has inherited and the influences of its environment.

Heterozygous: Having two different alleles at a given locus. Breeders often shorten this term to "het."

Homozygous: Having two identical alleles at a given locus.

Wild type: The phenotype most commonly seen in wild-caught individuals, usually considered the normal appearance. The allele at each locus that produces the wild-type phenotype.

Axanthic ball python. These ball pythons have a mutation that interferes with the production of yellow pigments.

Recessive: A mutant allele that changes the phenotype only when it occurs in the homozygous form. When heterozygous, the individual looks normal.

Codominant: A mutant allele that changes the phenotype when either homozygous or heterozygous. A heterozygous individual does not look like a homozygous individual, and neither does it look like a normal one.

Caramel albino ball python, also called a T-positive albino or a xanthic albino.

Dominant: An allele that changes the phenotype when either homozygous or heterozygous. A heterozygous individual looks like a homozygous individual.

Double heterozygous: Heterozygous at two gene loci.

Triple heterozygous: Heterozygous at three gene loci.

Punnett square: A learning tool for determining the possible outcomes of a given cross between individuals. It was developed by R.C. Punnett, an early British geneticist.

Symbols

Some of the names used to describe various color and pattern mutations are rather long. For example, the name "lavender albino" contains 14 letters. Using the entire word when filling in a Punnett square would make it enormous. Abbreviations or symbols are used instead of the entire name when describing the mutation. Mendel originated some of the rules used for symbolizing today. The rules are as follows:

1. The symbol is a unique, one- to four-letter abbreviation of the *mutant name*. For example, *a* could be used for albino. As *a* is already taken, *ax* could be used for axanthic.
2. All characters in a recessive mutant's symbol are lower case. Again, *a* is for albino, a recessive mutation.
3. All characters in a dominant or codominant mutant's symbol are lower case, except for the first letter, which is upper case. For example, *Pa* could stand for pastel, a codominant mutant in the ball python.
4. The symbol of the locus is the same as the symbol for the first mutant gene found at that locus. For example, *a* stands for both the albino mutant gene and the albino's locus. *Pa* stands for both the pastel mutant gene and the pastel's locus.
5. The symbol of the wild-type or normal allele at each locus is the locus symbol followed by a plus sign as a superscript. For example, the wild-type allele at the *a* locus would be a^+. The wild-type allele at the *Pa* locus would be Pa^+. If usage is clear, the wild-type allele can be symbolized by a plus sign alone.
6. As genes come in pairs—one from the father and one from the mother—there are two alleles in a genotype. The two symbols may be separated by two slash marks (//), particularly in complicated genotypes. While useful, the slash marks are optional. For example, an albino individual could be symbolized as either $a//a$ or aa. A heterozygous pastel could be either $Pa//Pa^+$ or $PaPa^+$.
7. The more dominant allele goes on the left side of the genotype, and the more recessive allele goes on the right side of the genotype. For example, a heterozygous albino would be a^+a.
8. Always remember to clearly label all the symbols used in your Punnett squares.

Setting up Your Punnett Squares

A Punnett square is a useful tool for figuring out the chances of getting a desired phenotype from a breeding. Being able to set one up and understand its use will aid you in determining which pairs of your pythons are most likely to produce the offspring you want. They can also help you determine what types you might need to purchase to further your breeding endeavors and can even help you figure out the genetics of snakes when the genotype is unknown.

In most cells, the chromosomes come in pairs. During the development of the gametes (sperm and egg cells), the chromosome pairs separate. Half of the chromosomes will go to one gamete and the other half will go to another gamete.

Example One: Single Recessive Trait
Albino × Normal

For the following example, we will use a breeding between an albino and a normal, also written as albino × normal. The albino is represented by aa (two recessive alleles) and the normal, wild type, is represented by a^+a^+ (two normal or dominant alleles). The cross is written $aa \times a^+a^+$. The two possible gametes from one parent are listed across the top of the Punnett square and the two possible gametes from the other parent are listed down the side of the Punnett square. When setting up the square, each allele needs to be placed over or next to its corresponding box.

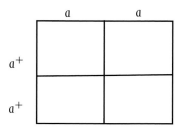

Remember, there are two alleles for each trait. Hence aa for albino. In a normal ball python, the albino allele is not present, only the wild-type allele. This allele is indicated through using a^+a^+. Once everything is in place, the square can be completed. The letters on the left are brought across to the squares that are in their row. The letters on the top are brought down and placed beside the letters in their columns.

	a	a
a^+	a^+a	a^+a
a^+	a^+a	a^+a

The resulting offspring are all heterozygous for the albino trait; however, they all look like normal ball pythons. Ball pythons that are heterozygous for a recessive mutant gene display the normal phenotype.

Example Two: Double Recessive Cross
Heterozygous Albino × Heterozygous Axanthic

In this example, the two parents are heterozygous for two different recessive alleles, albino (a) and axanthic (ax). Both appear normal, but are carrying the recessive genes for both phenotypes. Genetically speaking, this cross can be represented as $a^+aax^+ax \times a^+aax^+ax$.

This Punnett square is set up similarly to the last one except that it is expanded to make room for two different genes.

	a^+ax^+	a^+ax	aax^+	aax
a^+ax^+	$a^+a^+ax^+ax^+$	$a^+a^+ax^+ax$	$a^+aax^+ax^+$	a^+aax^+ax
a^+ax	$a^+a^+ax^+ax$	a^+a^+axax	a^+aax^+ax	a^+aaxax
aax^+	$a^+aax^+ax^+$	$a^+aax^+ax^+$	$aaax^+ax^+$	$aaax^+ax^+$
aax	a^+aax^+ax	a^+aaxax	$aaax^+ax$	$aaaxax$

In this cross, 6.25% of the offspring are normal ($a^+a^+ax^+ax^+$), 12.5% of the offspring are heterozygous for axanthic ($a^+a^+ax^+ax$), 12.5% of the offspring are heterozygous for albino ($a^+aax^+ax^+$), 25% of the offspring are heterozygous for albino and heterozygous for axanthic (a^+aax^+ax), 6.25% of the offspring are axanthic (a^+a^+axax), 12.5% of the offspring are axanthic heterozygous for albino (a^+aaxax), 6.25% of the offspring are albino ($aaax^+ax^+$), 12.5% of the offspring are albino heterozygous axanthic ($aaax^+ax$), and 6.25% of the offspring are homozygous for albino and axanthic ($aaaxax$). Another way to look at it

Lavender albino. This is another form of albinism different from both the albino and the caramel albino.

is this way: 1 of 16 is $a^+a^+ax^+ax^+$ normal, 2 of 16 are $a^+a^+ax^+ax$ heterozygous for axanthic, 2 of 16 are $a^+aax^+ax^+$ heterozygous for albino, 4 of 16 are a^+aax^+ax heterozygous for albino and heterozygous for axanthic, 1 of 16 is a^+a^+axax axanthic, 2 of 16 are a^+aaxax axanthic heterozygous for albino, 1 of 16 is $aaax^+ax^+$ albino, 2 of 16 are $aaax^+ax$ albino heterozygous for axanthic, and last but not least, 1 of 16 is $aaaxax$ homozygous for albino and homozygous for axanthic, also known as a snow ball python.

The above may be a bit tedious to read through, but it lays down a very important foundation for future breeding projects. The represented diagrams should be enough, along with the text, to give you a good basic understanding of how the crosses work genetically and how you set up and use the Punnett square. It is important not to take short cuts when setting up your Punnett squares, as it will not accurately represent the odds, especially in more complicated crosses involving multiple genetic mutations.

When breeding a heterozygous ball python to another ball python that is also heterozygous for the same genetic mutation, the odds are 1 in 4 that you will produce the mutation.

Piebald ball python. The amount of white coloration on these animals is highly variable.

In a cross involving double heterozygous simple recessive (two genes) mutations, the odds are 1 in 16 that you will produce the desired cross. In a triple heterozygous simple recessive (three genes) cross, the odds are 1 in 64 that you will produce the desired cross! Now all this is when you use simple recessive mutations. When codominants or dominants are thrown into the mix, the odds change. Understanding how the genetics affect the outcome of potential projects is essential to the success of that project.

Odds

When a Punnett square is completed, it illustrates a statistical average for the results; however, many clutches do not hatch out according to those averages. The Punnett square is a guide to *possible* results, not a guarantee of results. For example, a cross between an albino and a heterozygous albino should result in 50% of the hatchlings being albino and the other 50% being heterozygous for albino; however this is an ideal ratio. In actuality, a clutch consisting of 6 eggs may hatch out 5 albinos and 1 heterozygous albino. A second clutch consisting of 5 eggs may hatch out 1 albino and 4 heterozygous albinos. In one instance, one of our clutches hatched out more albinos than expected, and another clutch hatched out less than expected. It is also important to remember that the odds apply to each egg in the clutch. Many times, the odds incorrectly are applied to the clutch as a whole, instead of to each egg individually. Please keep this in mind when your clutches hatch.

Morphs

Ball python color and pattern mutations are also known as morphs. Many of the color and pattern mutations seen today came into the United States from Africa. Once they reached the United States, a few dedicated and enterprising breeders purchased these snakes and took the time to care for them until they were able to get them to successfully reproduce. More than 30 morphs have been brought into the United States from Africa over the past several years, and each year brings the possibility of yet another previously unseen new and unique morph. Ball pythons have had more unique color and pattern mutations brought into captivity over the years than any other reptile species. This may be due to the large numbers of ball pythons that are collected and hatched on an annual basis in Africa.

Often, several years must pass before any of the newest morphs are available for purchase. It is not uncommon for a breeder to take several years to work out the inheritance of a new mutation. The first morph that was successfully reproduced in captivity, back in May of 1992, was the albino ball python, and that one started it all.

Designer morphs are created in captivity by breeding different morphs together to produce a new and unique-looking ball python. The first of these designer morphs to

Hybrids

A hybrid is produced when two separate species are bred together to produce a new type of (in this case) snake. Some hybrids are fertile, and some are not. Usually, fertile hybrids are created when the number of chromosomes from one parent is the same as the number of chromosomes from the other parent. Some people really enjoy hybrids; others do not care for them at all. One of the biggest potential problems with hybrids is the failure to properly disclose the genetic makeup of the snake. This may cause tremendous problems in the future when individuals may acquire snakes that they think are, for example, pure Angolan pythons, and after breeding trials and further research, they discover that they are not. This could really disrupt an individual's breeding project, hard work, finances, and time.

Three hybrids have been produced to date using ball pythons. There is a blood ball, which is a hybrid between a ball python and a blood python; an Angolan ball, which is a hybrid between an Angolan python and a ball python; and last, the Burm ball, which is a hybrid between a Burmese python and a ball python.

be produced in captivity was the snow ball python. The snow was produced by breeding together two previously established mutations: an albino (a ball python lacking black pigment) to an axanthic (a ball python lacking yellow pigment). Their subsequent offspring (which all looked normal in appearance but contained one copy each of the albino gene and axanthic gene) were reared to maturity and then bred back to each other. Since the appearance of the snow ball in 2001, well over 75 new designer ball python morphs have been produced, with dozens more on the horizon. With the tremendous number of morphs to work with, the number of potential designer morphs is absolutely staggering.

The clown morph results from a simple recessive mutation of the pattern.

Since there are such a tremendous number of possible color and pattern combinations for the ball python, it is not feasible for any published work to list them all. By the time the book would be published, there could be as many as 30 more new morphs. Here, we take a look at some of the more common and popular morphs available today.

Simple Recessives

Albino Albino ball pythons technically are amelanistic ball pythons. The term amelanistic means "lacking melanin." Melanin is the pigment responsible for blacks and browns. Albino ball pythons are yellow and white with red eyes. The yellow can vary from pale to dark mustard. Albino ball pythons have normal patterns; only the color has been modified in this

Do Your Research

Dozens and dozens of different colors and patterns of ball pythons are available today. If you plan on breeding, it is extremely important that you clearly understand the genetics behind each morph. This understanding will enable you to make better decisions with your breeding projects.

When albino snakes have some black coloration, they are called paradox albinos. This is a paradox caramel albino.

morph. Occasionally, an albino ball python will hatch with random black scales or patches of normal coloring on it. These types of albinos are often referred to as paradox albinos. The term "paradox" is used to describe the patches of normal coloration that occasionally occur with different color morphs. The albino ball python was the first morph successfully reproduced in captivity.

Axanthic The term *axanthic* means "lacking yellow pigment"—the yellow pigment is called xanthin. Axanthic balls pythons are typically black, white, and gray. Some axanthic ball pythons have a brown hue to them. Some are light silver, while others are a very dark gray. At least three lines of axanthic ball pythons exist, and these lines are not compatible with one another. The three lines are the Joliff line, the VPI line, and the TSK line.

When incompatible lines are bred together, no visual morphs will be produced, only double heterozygous animals. This is due to the allele for the color or pattern being located on a different locus for each line; these alleles do not line up with one another. Axanthics of other lines have also been brought into the country from time to time. Presently, it is not known if any of the newer axanthic

Genetic striped ball python. Striping can also be caused by fluctuating incubation temperatures and other factors.

Genetic banded ball python. This is one of the newer morphs.

lines are compatible with the original three established lines. *Paradox axanthics* also have been produced. These have very noticeable patches of yellow pigment on them. Axanthic ball pythons have normal patterns, only the color is abnormal.

Caramel Albino Caramel albino ball pythons are also known as xanthic albinos and as T-positive—usually written as T+—albinos. A protein called tyrosinase is required for the synthesis of melanin. When tyrosinase is absent, it produces a T− albino or an amelanistic ball python. When the protein functions in small amounts, it produces a different type of albino, such as the caramel albino. Since the protein is present in small amounts, it allows for the partial synthesis of melanin and this is what influences the color of the T+ albino.

Some caramel albinos will have areas of normal pigment. This is not unusual due to the presence of tyrosinase. Caramel albino ball pythons are golden brown, yellow, and orange with red pupils. Unfortunately, a percentage of caramel albino ball pythons hatch out with spinal kinks. It is not yet known why this happens with this morph. Hopefully, through more selective breeding efforts, the number of kinked animals produced will decrease.

Hypomelanistic Hypomelanistic means a reduction in melanin; *hypo-* means low or under. The reduction of melanin in these snakes gives them a lighter than normal color. The colors on hypomelanistic ball pythons are muted. This type of color morph has also been referred to as a *ghost ball python*. Many hypomelanistic ball pythons seem to exhibit particular color shades. These are commonly referred to as *orange ghosts*, *yellow ghosts*, and *green ghosts*. Many hypomelanistic lines are compatible with one another, but some lines are incompatible. When purchasing a hypomelanistic ball python, clarify with the seller if the snake you are purchasing is compatible with other hypomelanistic lines. The hypomelanistic gene has proven to be very useful in producing new and cleaner color combinations. When it has been combined with other genetic mutations, it has produced some truly spectacular color combinations. "Hypo" is the term commonly used for this morph instead of the longer hypomelanistic.

Lavender Albino Lavender albino ball pythons are also a form of T+ albino. The lavender albino is a fairly new morph and has only been available for a few years. As hatchlings, they are a bright yellow orange with light lavender markings instead of white. This lavender coloring is visible on most hatchlings. The eyes of the lavender albino are a ruby red color. As lavender albinos age, their colors deepen and change. They mature into very spectacularly colored adults, with the lavender becoming deeper and much more noticeable and the yellow-orange becoming a vibrant orange color.

Piebald This simple recessive mutation affects both color and pattern. The term *piebald* has been used for years to describe black and white horses, and it turned out to be the perfect term for this color and pattern

Pastel jungle is a codominant mutation. When it is heterozygous, the snake is a pastel jungle (top). When it is homozygous, the snake will be a superpastel (bottom).

mutation. Piebald ball pythons are truly unique in the reptile world. No other reptile has the pure white of the piebald matched against the normal body color. No two piebald ball pythons have the same pattern. They can range from having a small percentage of white that only covers the belly of the snake to as much as 95 percent white, where only the head and neck areas are normally colored. The normally colored areas of the piebald ball python are not normally patterned. Many times, dual stripes are present that run on either side of the backbone. In hatchlings, the normally colored areas are often bordered by a vibrant orange. The amount of white that appears on a piebald when it hatches is the amount of white it will have as an adult; the snake will not gain more white as it ages. The pattern will not change. Occasionally, black scales will randomly appear in the white areas of the snake as it matures.

The Mojave (top) and butter (bottom) morphs are similar in appearance and both can be used to produce white, blue-eyed snakes.

Clown Produced by another simple recessive mutation affecting pattern and color, the appearance of the clown ball python is very distinctive. The head has beautiful markings on it, and the dark background color is fused into a vertebral stripe that begins at the base of the skull and travels down the back of the snake to the tip of the tail. Occasionally, lines branch from the vertebral stripe down the sides of the snake. The lighter color of the clown ball python is a nice golden yellow. Many breeders have selectively bred a variety of clown that does not have the side patterning. This type of pattern on a clown is referred to as *reduced-pattern clown*. As clown ball pythons age, the very dark markings on them become lighter, giving the snake the appearance of being a two-toned golden snake.

Genetic Stripe The genetic stripe morph was eagerly anticipated by breeders, and it became available around 2000. Genetic stripes' patterns can range from a nice, even, complete vertebral stripe to a broken stripe in some cases, producing a blocky-looking pattern. The stripe down the back is golden and is often bordered by very dark brown stripes. The sides are also a beautiful golden brown. Some genetic stripes have faint markings on the sides, usually in the shape of a diamond. Some genetic stripes have very reduced dark lines bordering the vertebral stripe whereas, in other examples, these stripes are almost completely absent.

Genetic Banded Genetic bandeds are great-looking ball pythons. They have nice, wide, gold bands that are bordered by thin black lines. The pattern is fairly even on the snake. The overall appearance of the snake is very clean with no black flecking on the sides. Some of them even have scales that have a noticeably different feel when they are touched. The genetic banded is also a relative newcomer to the ball python scene. This morph has tremendous potential: Breeding it to many of the existing color morphs may create beautifully colored ball pythons with a fabulous banded pattern.

Ivory ball pythons begin life with a lot of yellow coloration, which fades as the snake ages.

Codominants and Dominants

In simple recessive mutations, the heterozygous form of the morph visibly looks like a normal-colored ball python, but it carries the gene for the desired morph. In a dominant or codominant morph, the heterozygous form is visibly different from a normal-colored ball python. These are often referred to as *visible heterozygous ball pythons*. When in the homozygous form, a codominant's color and or pattern is visibly different from the heterozygous form, which is also different from a normal-colored and -patterned ball python. In dominant morphs, the heterozygous form and homozygous form look the same and can only be distinguished through breeding trials. At this time, there are at least 30 different codominant and dominant ball python morphs.

Pastel Jungle The pastel jungle was the first codominant ball python mutation to be discovered. It looks distinctly different from a normal ball python. Pastel jungle ball pythons have bright yellow-orange where the normal gold areas are generally found on a ball python and dark black coloring. Some lines of pastels have lots of highlights or *blushing* in their dark colors. The homozygous form of the pastel jungle is called a *super pastel*. They have very pale lavender-colored heads and nice, clean, light yellow markings as hatchlings. As they mature, some super pastels become very yellow, while others will be more orange. Selective breeding has produced some lines of super pastels that have very high fading or blushing along the top of the snake, producing a "bleached out" appearance. This fading leaves the center

> The cinnamon morph lacks yellow, making a reddish-brown snake.

portions almost white, with the coloration gradually darkening toward the edges.

Mojave Mojave ball pythons have a very distinctive pattern that has more striping than is seen in normally patterned ball pythons. Mojave ball pythons also have a distinct green look to them. They are white,

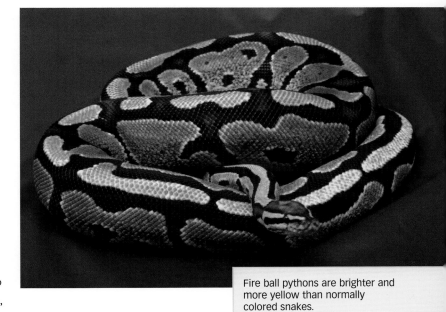

Fire ball pythons are brighter and more yellow than normally colored snakes.

dark brown, and yellow-green or light yellow. When two Mojaves are bred together, the odds are one in four that a super Mojave or a homozygous Mojave will be produced. Super Mojaves are white snakes with dark grey heads and light blue eyes.

Two other morphs that are similar to the Mojave in appearance are the *butter morph* and the *lesser morph*. The butter and lesser have slightly different hues to their color and are lighter than the Mojave in appearance. They are yellow, light brown, and white. Both, when bred to themselves, will produce white, blue-eyed snakes. White, blue-eyed babies are also produced when ball pythons are bred to each other in one of these pairings: Mojave × lesser, butter × Mojave, or lesser × butter. These white, blue-eyed ball pythons produced from breeding the two different morphs together may look like supers, but they are not. A super lesser or super Mojave, when bred to a normal, will produce all lessers and all Mojaves respectively. When one of the blue-eyed, white, non-supers from, for example, a butter × lesser is bred to a normal, it will produce butters and lessers.

Ivory As adults, ivory ball pythons are beautiful. They have light lavender-colored heads with a light yellow vertebral stripe that runs from the neck down to the tip of the tail. Often, this stripe is bordered by a thin lavender line. The rest of the ball python is white. As a hatchling,

The genetics of the banana morph are not fully understood, but it is probably a dominant mutation.

ivory ball pythons have a lot of color. They are white with a distinct head pattern and bright yellow vertebral stripe. As the snake ages, more and more colored scales begin to appear on the dorsal surface. These scales are orange, yellow, and lavender. By the time the snake is two years old, the color has faded and the yellow vertebral stripe is all that is left, along with the light lavender head markings. The heterozygous form of the ivory is referred to as a *yellow belly* or a *het ivory*. These heterozygous animals also have a unique appearance. Many of them have bright yellow random scales, a mottled pattern on the edge of the belly scales, and coloring that is different from normal.

Cinnamon Cinnamon ball pythons are the opposite of pastel jungle ball pythons. Instead of having an increase in yellow, they are almost completely without yellow. Cinnamon ball pythons are a reddish brown and dark brown. Their patterns are also different from that of a normal ball python. Many cinnamons exhibit more of a striping pattern than a normal ball python. As cinnamon ball pythons age, they lose some of the red hue that they had as hatchlings. The homozygous form of the cinnamon ball python is a very dark brown, almost black, ball python. Super cinnamons occasionally have flecks of lighter color on them in random areas.

When a cinnamon is bred to a black pastel (a different codominant morph that is similar to the cinnamon), the offspring will look like super cinnamons: they will be black or very dark brown. The super form of the black pastel is also a very dark, almost black ball python. As with the Mojave-lesser-butter complex, the breeding of one of these very dark ball pythons produced from a black pastel × cinnamon to a normal will produce black pastels and cinnamons.

Fire Fire ball pythons are the heterozygous form of what is referred to as the *black-eyed leucistic*. Fire ball pythons are lighter and brighter in color than normal ball pythons. They tend to be more yellow in color with light spots on the top of the head. When two fires are bred together, they produce a homozygous ball python that is white with black eyes. Occasionally these ball pythons will have random spots of pale yellow on them. Even though the eye is black, the color of the pupil is red. Fires have been bred into several different morphs, and they "cleaned" up the coloring and appearance of some of the morphs that they have been bred into.

Banana Banana ball pythons are truly spectacular looking. They are a form of albino, but they are not simple recessive; they seem to be a dominant mutation. At the time of this writing, the banana has not been proven to be codominant. Banana ball pythons are lavender and orange with random black flecks

Spider ball python. This morph has been combined with many others to produce unique and beautiful pythons.

on their bodies. They are similar to the lavender albino ball python in color, but the lavender lacks black flecking. The banana ball python has tremendous potential to produce numerous new and colorful ball pythons.

Spider The spider morph is a dominant pattern mutation. At this time, no known homozygous spider ball pythons exist. These snakes have very unique markings. The black or dark brown coloring is reduced down to very thin lines that cross the back and run down the sides of the snake into the side coloring. A spider ball python often has lots of white coming up from the bottom into the gold coloring. Many times, the white will continue up higher onto the body. The white coloring is not found in the black or dark brown areas of the spider ball python, and the amount of white will vary from spider to spider. The lighter color is a nice light gold and in some cases a clean yellow color. Spider ball pythons often have black flecking on their labials and distinctive head markings. This morph is very popular and has been used to make many new ball python morphs.

Some spider ball pythons have wobbly heads and an inability to strike straight. Good breeders will not sell spiders that demonstrate this problem in the extreme.

Pinstripe This is a dominant color and pattern mutation. Pinstripe ball pythons have fine dark brown lines that form various random patterns that weave through the gold background. Pinstripes do not have patterns on the head like spider ball or clown ball pythons. However, they do have light-colored heads.

The amount of white on sugar ball pythons varies considerably.

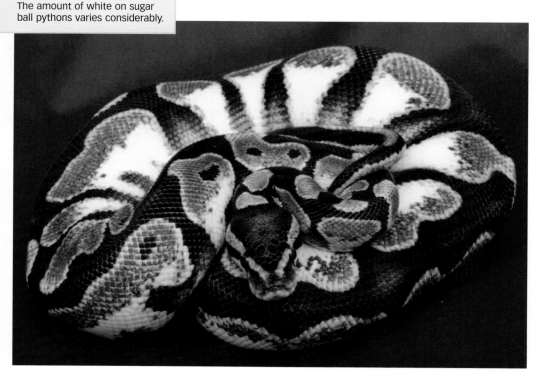

The snow ball python is homozygous for both albino and axanthic mutations.

Pinstripes have very unique and cryptic markings, and they have also been used to create some very new and exciting color combinations. At this time, no known homozygous pinstripe ball pythons exist. Refer to the photo at the start of this chapter to see a pinstripe ball python.

Sugar The sugar ball python morph originated in Europe and was brought into the United States by a few breeders. They are a predominantly black-backed ball python with white coming up their sides. The amount of white varies from individual to individual; some have a lot of white coming up the sides and are just spectacular, while some have only a moderate amount. This is a dominant mutation, and at this time, no known homozygous sugar ball pythons exist. *Calicos* are another morph that is very similar in appearance to the sugar, but their pattern is much more random.

Designer Ball Pythons

A designer ball python is produced by combing two or more different color or color-and-pattern mutations together to produce a new and unique looking ball python. Hundreds of combinations are possible, and many dozens of designer ball pythons have already been produced. Each year brings more new and interesting looking ball pythons. As mentioned earlier, there is no limit to the possible combinations; the only potential limiting factor is your imagination.

Double recessives are very difficult to produce because the odds of producing the desired cross are 1 in 16. Few of these types of designer ball pythons have been produced. Some of the combinations that have been made include lavender albino piebald, axanthic clown, albino clown, hypomelanistic caramel albino, albino genetic stripe, and hypomelanistic piebald.

The designer ball pythons that are created using a simple recessive mutation and a dominant or codominant mutation are simpler to produce than the straight simple recessive only combinations. The odds are better for these types of crosses, especially if you use the homozygous form of the simple recessive mutation. Many interesting and wonderful crosses have been produced by combining simple recessives and codominants or dominants.

The hypo Mojave (above) combines the hypomelanistic and Mojave mutations. Taking it one step further is the hypo spider Mojave (below).

The designer ball pythons created by breeding codominants to each other—by breeding them to dominants or by breeding dominants together—are by far the simplest types of designer ball pythons to produce. Instead of your odds being 1 in 16 to produce the desired cross, your odds improve greatly since the heterozygous snakes used are visible heterozygous animals. Your odds are 1 in 4 to produce the desired cross! Much better odds than the 1 in 16 encountered by breeding simple recessives. Dozens of these types of designer morphs have been produced.

Crossing a pastel jungle ball python with a spider results in a bumblebee morph.

Even when using three different color or color-and-pattern mutations, the crosses are easier to produce since the odds are so much more favorable. Very often, the results of such crosses are completely unexpected, with the colors and patterns blending in unanticipated ways.

The killer clown ball python is the result of breeding a pastel clown to a pastel clown.

Snow The snow ball was the first double recessive color mutation to be produced. This wonderful ball python is the result of combining the simple recessive traits of the albino and the axanthic. Snow ball pythons from the VPI line and the TSK line get whiter as the age. They also have light pink eyes and are just absolutely unreal looking snakes.

Hypo Mojave This is the result of a cross between a codominant and a simple recessive mutation. A hypo Mojave is a hypomelanistic Mojave. A hypo Mojave combines the traits of the heterozygous Mojave ball python with the homozygous hypomelanistic ball python. Hypo Mojaves go through a color change from hatchling to adulthood. As hatchlings, they have much more of an orange cast to them. As adults, they are a clean yellow-green, white, and gray. When a hypo Mojave is bred to a normal, you will produce Mojaves heterozygous for hypomelanism and heterozygous hypomelanistic ball pythons.

Killer Clown A killer clown is a super pastel clown. Here is a double homozygous ball python using a simple recessive trait and a codominant trait. Killer clowns combine the best of both worlds: the great pattern of the clown with the fabulous colors of a super pastel jungle. The head pattern of the killer clown is highly

Several different crosses can produce the stunning killer blast morph.

reduced and is a very light color with flecks on it. The yellow is bright and clean, and the vertebral stripe is a lavender color. When a killer clown is bred to a normal, it produces pastel jungles heterozygous for clown ball pythons.

Bumblebee Bumblebees are stunning ball pythons that have enjoyed enormous popularity. They are produced by breeding a pastel jungle to a spider (dominant × codominant). Both the spider and the pastel jungle are in the heterozygous form in this morph. Bumblebees are yellow, white, and dark brown and are very beautiful ball pythons. When a bumblebee is bred to a normal, it can produce spiders, pastels, normals, and bumblebees.

Killer Blast A killer blast is a super pastel pinstripe (dominant × codominant). A killer blast can be produced by breeding a lemon blast (pastel pinstripe) to a super pastel or from breeding a lemon blast to a lemon blast. Killer blasts are a bright, clean yellow, white, and lavender. Some other combinations could potentially produce a killer blast, but the most common are those listed. When a killer blast is bred to a normal, the breeding can produce pastel jungles and lemon blasts. Since the super pastel jungle portion of the designer morph is the homozygous form, all of the offspring will be at the very least pastel jungles. The portion that would hatch out as pinstripes will be lemon blasts, since both traits would be combined.

Mojave Bee A Mojave bee is a Mojave pastel spider (dominant × codominant × codominant). Here is a triple combination that once again is much simpler to create when using the dominant or codominant morphs than it would be by using only simple recessives. This cross was a pleasant surprise for us, as it hatched out much prettier than we ever could have anticipated. The Mojave traits cleaned up the bumblebee, brightened up the yellow, and changed the pattern. Mojave bees can be produced by crossing a Mojave and a bumblebee.

You can produce a Mojave bee by breeding a Mojave to a bumblebee.

The black-striped ball python was recently proven to be a simple recessive mutation.

 *Glossary*

caudal: relating to or near the tail.

cloaca: the common *ventral* opening behind the back legs from which genital, intestinal, and urinary tracts exit the body. The cloaca actually refers to the internal area within the *vent* rather than the opening itself, but is often used interchangeably with the *vent*.

clutch: a group of eggs laid by the same female at the same time.

dorsal: relating to the top or back region of an animal.

dystocia: also called *egg-binding*; the situation in which an animal has difficulty laying eggs or giving birth.

ectoparasite: any parasitic organism that is found on the skin of the host organism and attaches itself to feed on the host's blood, e.g. mites and ticks.

ectotherm: an animal that depends on the temperature of its surroundings to regulate its body temperature.

egg-binding: also called *dystocia*; the situation in which an animal has difficulty laying eggs or giving birth.

egg tooth: a small, toothlike projection on the snout of fetal reptiles used to break out of the egg; the egg tooth falls off shortly after hatching.

endoparasite: any parasitic organism that lives inside of the host, e.g. tapeworms.

gravid: the condition in which an animal is carrying developing eggs, whether fertile or infertile.

hatchling: a young reptile that has hatched out of its egg relatively recently; it is usually applied to individuals that less than six months old but it is an inexact term.

hemipenes: the male snake's mating organ; called such because it is a paired apparatus; each is called a hemipenis.

herp: term for reptiles and amphibians collectively, derived from *herpetology*.

herpetoculturist: an individual who studies the captive care and husbandry of reptiles and amphibians.

herpetologist: an individual who studies the branch of zoology comprising reptiles and amphibians.

herpetology: the branch of zoology comprising reptiles and amphibians.

impaction: condition in which some material—often the cage substrate—is obstructing the digestive tract.

Jacobson's organ: sensory apparatus at the roof of a snake's mouth that detects chemicals (scents) brought in by the forked tongue. Also called the *vomeronasal organ*.

juvenile: a young herp that has not reached sexual maturity.

labial pits: indentations on the lips of pythons that are sensitive to heat, enabling the snake to detect warm-blooded prey in the dark.

morph: physical differences from the normal or wild-type animals. In ball pythons, most morphs are genetic differences in color and/or pattern, and breeders have crossed the various morphs to create ball python varieties that do not exist in nature (called *designer morphs*).

neonate: newly hatched baby snake.

oviposition: the process of laying eggs.

Salmonella: a genus of bacteria that occurs naturally in the gut of most reptiles. If transmitted in high concentrations to humans can lead to serious health problems particularly in immuno-compromised individuals. Often used as a synonym for *salmonellosis*.

salmonellosis: the digestive illness caused by *Salmonella*.

spur: small protuberance on each side of the vent used by male pythons in courtship.

thermoregulation: altering body temperature to the preferred temperature; pythons are *ectotherms* and they thermoregulate by using warm or cool areas in their environment.

vent: the actual opening where waste products from the *cloaca* are expelled from the body, and from which the male extrudes his *hemipenis* during mating. It can be seen as a slit on the underside of the tail.

ventral: the underside or belly. This, naturally enough, is where you'll find the *vent*.

vomeronasal organ: sensory apparatus at the roof of a snakes's mouth that detects chemicals (scents) brought in by the forked tongue. Also called the *Jacobson's organ*.

zoonosis: a disease that can pass from animals to humans, e.g. *salmonella*.

References

Barker, Dave G. and Tracy M. *Pythons of the World, Volume II: Ball Pythons.* Gardena: VPI Library, 2006.

Broghammer, Stefan. *Ball Pythons Habitat, Care and Breeding.* Trossingen: M&S Reptilien Verlag, 2001.

Carmichael, Rob. Maternal Incubation of the Ball Python *Python regius. BallPython.Snakes.Net.* http://ballpython.snakes.net/robcarmichael/maternal.htm (9 Nov 2004)

Clark, Bob. Python Color and Pattern Morphs. *Reptiles.* March 1996, pp. 56-67.

de Vosjoli, Philippe; Klingenberg, Roger; Barker, Dave and Tracy. *The Ball Python Manual.* Singapore: Advanced Vivarium Systems, 1995.

Sutherland, Colette. Genetically Speaking. *The Snake Keeper.* http://ballpython.com/page.php?topic=genetically (3 Nov 2004)

Clubs and Societies

American Society of Ichthyologists and Herpetologists
Maureen Donnelly, Secretary
Grice Marine Laboratory
Florida International University
Biological Sciences
11200 SW 8th St.
Miami, FL 33199
Telephone: (305) 348-1235
E-mail: asih@fiu.edu
www.asih.org

Amphibian, Reptile & Insect Association
Liz Price
23 Windmill Rd
Irthlingsborough
Wellingborough NN9 5RJ
England

Society for the Study of Amphibians and Reptiles (SSAR)
Marion Preest, Secretary
The Claremont Colleges
925 N. Mills Ave.
Claremont, CA 91711
Phone: 909-607-8014
E-mail: mpreest@jsd.clare-mont.edu
www.ssarherps.org

Web Resources

HerpNetwork
www.herpnetwork.com

Herpo.com listing of herpetological societies
www.herpo.com/societies.html

Kingsnake
www.kingsnake.com

Kingsnake (UK)
www.kingsnake.co.uk

Resource for feeding issues
www.anapsid.org/ballfeed.html

The Snake Keeper (author's site)
www.ballpython.com

A Troubleshooting Guide to Ball Pythons
www.kingsnake.com/ballpythonguide/

Veterinary Resources

Association of Reptile and Amphibian Veterinarians
P.O. Box 605
Chester Heights, PA 19017
Phone: 610-358-9530
Fax: 610-892-4813
E-mail: ARAVETS@aol.com
www.arav.org

Rescue And Adoption Services

Las Cruces Reptile Rescue
www.awesomereptiles.com/lcrr/rescueorgs.html

New England Amphibian and Reptile Rescue
www.ReptileRescue.net

Petfinder.com
www.petfinder.org

Reptile Rescue, Canada
http://www.reptilerescue.o
n.ca/

Magazines

Reptilia
Salvador Mundi 2
Spain-08017 Barcelona
E-mail: Subscripciones-sub-
scriptions@reptilia.org

Reptile Care
Mulberry Publications, Ltd.
Suite 209 Wellington House
Butt Road, Colchester
Essex, CO3 3DA
United Kingdom

Reptiles Magazine
P.O. Box 6050
Mission Viejo, CA 92690
www.animalnetwork.com/
reptiles

Photo Credits:

Index

of hatchlings, 90–91
live or prekilled food, 49–51
natural diet, 11
prey item types, 48
prey size, 48–49
problems with, 8, 14, 48, 52–53, 59–62
vacations and, 53
females. *See* breeding females
fertilization, 81–82
fire morph, **109**, 111
genetic banded morph, **104**, 107
genetic stripe morph, **103**, 107
genetics, 93–101. *See also* morphs
    odds, 97–98
    Punnett squares, 95, 97–100
    symbols, 95–96
    terms, 94–95
gestation, 81–82
ghost morph, 105
gravid, defined, 118
habitat, natural, 6–8
handling, 40–42, 60–61
hatching, **87**, 89–90
hatching season, 7–8
hatchlings, **8**, 8, 19, 90–91, **91**, 119
health care, 55–73
    diarrhea, 68–69
    egg retention, 72, 118
    external parasites, 20–22, 57–59, 118
    failure to eat, 48, 52–53, 59–62
    hemipene infection, **70**, 70–71
    internal parasites, 57, 118, 123
    mouth rot, **69**, 69–70
    new snake assessment, 18–22
    prolapse, 71
    regurgitation, 66–67
    resources on, 123
    respiratory infections, 20, 65–66

retained shed, 67–68
rodent bites, 49–50, **64**, 64–65
rubbed noses, 72–73
Salmonella, 73, 120
spinal injuries, 71–72
thermal burns, 62–64
veterinarian selection, 56
yolk remnant removal, 19
heat cables, 30
heat-sensing pits, labial, 10, **10**, 119
heat tape, **30**
heating, 29–31
hemipenal prolapse, 71
hemipene infection, **70**, 70–71
hemipenes, 119
herp, 119
herp expos, 17
herpetoculturist, 119
herpetological societies, 15, 21, 123
herpetologist, 119
herpetology, 119
het ivory morph, 110
heterozygous, 94–95
hibernation, 78
hide boxes, **33**, 35–36
homozygous, 95
housing, 25–45
    cage furnishings, 35–39
    cage types, **27**, 27–29, **28**, **34**
    cleaning, 39–40
    escapes, 42–43
    heating, 29–31
    humidity, 33–34
    lighting, 32–33
    placement of, 32–33
    security, 26
    size of, 26–27
    substrate, 34–35
humidity, 33–34
husbandry issues, and failure to feed, 60
hybrids, 101

hygiene, 67, 73
hypo Mojave morph, **114**, 115
hypomelanistic morph, **96**, 104–105
illnesses. *See* health care
impaction, 119
imported pythons, 8, 14, 59–60
incubation media, 84
incubation of eggs, 83–89
incubators, 84, 88–89
indoor/outdoor carpeting substrate, 35
infectious stomatitis. *See* mouth rot
internal parasites, 57, 118
Internet purchase of ball pythons, 17–18
Internet resources, 123
ivory morph, **107**, 109–110
Jacobson's organ, 119
juvenile, 119
killer blast morph, **116**, 116–117
killer clown morph, **115**, 116
labial heat-sensing pits, 10, **10**, 119
Latin names, 9
lavender albinos, **99**, 105
legal considerations, 21
length, 10
lesser morph, 109
life span, 14, 16
lighting, 32–33
Linnaeus, Carl, 8
live food, 49–50
locus (loci), 94
magazines, 124
males. *See* breeding males
mating, 78–79, **79**
mites, 22, 37, 58–59, **59**
Mojave bee morph, 117, **117**
Mojave morph, **106**, 109, 115. *See also* hypo Mojave morph
morphs, 14, 101–117. *See also* names of specific morphs, e.g., piebald morph